get married

WHAT WOMEN CAN DO
TO HELP IT HAPPEN

CANDICE WATTERS

MOODY PUBLISHERS

CHICAGO

All Scripture quotations, unless otherwise indicated, are taken from the *Holy Bible, New International Version*®. NIV®. Copyright © 1973, 1978, 1984 by International Bible Society. Used by permission of Zondervan. All rights reserved.

Scripture quotations marked NASB are taken from the *New American Standard Bible*®, Copyright © 1960, 1962, 1963, 1968, 1971, 1972, 1973, 1975, 1977, 1995 by The Lockman Foundation. Used by permission. (www.Lockman.org)

Scripture quotations marked NKJV are taken from the *New King James Version*. Copyright © 1982 by Thomas Nelson, Inc. Used by permission. All rights reserved.

Scripture quotations marked ESV are taken from *The Holy Bible, English Standard Version*. Copyright © 2000, 2001 by Crossway Bibles, a division of Good News Publishers. Used by permission. All rights reserved.

Cover design: John Hamilton Design, www.johnhamiltondesign.com
Cover photo: Ted Slater, www.tedslater.com
Interior design: Julia Ryan | www.DesignByJulia.com
Images: © 2007 iStock.com, © 2007 JupiterImages Corporation

Library of Congress Cataloging-in-Publication Data

Watters, Candice.
    Get married : what women can do to help it happen / Candice Watters.
        p. cm.
    Includes bibliographical references.
    ISBN-13: 978-0-8024-5829-2
    ISBN-10: 0-8024-5829-7
    1. Marriage—Religious aspects—Christianity. 2. Single women—Conduct of life.
    3. Christian women—Conduct of life. I. Title.
    BV835.W375 2008
    248.4—dc22
                                                        2007039054

We hope you enjoy this book from Moody Publishers. Our goal is to provide high-quality, thought-provoking books and products that connect truth to your real needs and challenges. For more information on other books and products written and produced from a biblical perspective, go to www.moodypublishers.com or write to:

Moody Publishers
820 N. LaSalle Boulevard
Chicago, IL 60610

3 5 7 9 10 8 6 4

Printed in the United States of America

For Hu and Mary,
whose bold faith started the ball rolling

CONTENTS

ACKNOWLEDGMENTS

Every good book is a community effort. Without the distinct contributions of many people, this book wouldn't have become what it is.

Trading notes with other writers, I realize my experience with Moody Publishers has been exceptional. Thank you, Lisa Major, for asking the question, "Have you ever thought about writing a book?"; Steve Lyon, for your vision for this message; and Jennifer Lyell, for being the champion every writer dreams of finding in an editor.

Boundless.org was my proving ground, and I'm indebted to Focus on the Family, and especially Charlie Jarvis, for believing in it; Ted Slater and Motte Brown for nourishing it; and all the readers over the years who contributed their stories and questions to the vibrant Boundless community. Special thanks to Mark Hartwig and Tom Hess for your influence on my ability to do more with words.

A great number of researchers and writers led the way in renewing the cultural conversation about marriage. To those who offered me their time and insight: Scott Stanley, Wade Horn, Leon Kass, Danielle Crittenden, Gary Thomas, Emerson Eggerichs, Scott Croft, Michael Lawrence, Debbie Maken, and Carolyn McCulley, thank you all.

It's been a source of both joy and heartache to walk alongside friends at various stages in their pursuit of marriage. Thanks to each of you who gave permission to share parts of your stories in this book.

I'm humbled by the wealth of mentors God has sent my way over the years:

At Calvin College—Steve Simpson, Frank Speyers, and Lois Konyndyk
At Regent University—Hubert and Mary Morken

Through *Boundless* and my time in Colorado—Jay and Sandy Budziszewski, Paul and Phyllis Stanley, and Kurt and Olivia Bruner

Thank you all for your investment and faith.

My dream of writing a book someday began when I was little and stayed alive because I was blessed with a family who believed in me. Thanks, Dad, Mom, Katie, Kenny, Kelly, and Caleb. I also married into a family of true believers. I only wish Steve's dad, Jim, were still on earth with Stephanie to see this book go to print.

To Harrison and Zoe, thank you for having childlike faith to pray for a publisher. And to little Churchill, thanks for sitting on my lap while I single-handedly (literally) wrote much of this book. Now it's time to celebrate.

To Steve, my husband and best friend, you believed in me more than I believed in myself. Without you, this book wouldn't have been written; without our story there would be little to say; without your coaching, encouragement, and skill, it wouldn't be nearly as interesting to read. No small dreams.

Finally, thank You, Father, for Your faithfulness in each season of my life, for proving over and over Your ability to do exceedingly, abundantly more than I could ask or imagine.

Colorado Springs, CO
June 2007

Foreword

From Genesis to Revelation, the Bible presents a conception of marriage that goes far beyond what most persons have even imagined. Contrary to what one might read in many books or see on movie screens today, Scripture teaches that marriage is not primarily about our self-esteem and personal fulfillment, nor is it just one lifestyle option among others. The Bible is clear in presenting a picture of marriage that is rooted in the glory of God made evident in creation itself. The man and the woman are made for each other and the institution of marriage is given to humanity as both opportunity and obligation.

Moreover, the Bible assumes that marriage is normative for human beings, and the responsibilities, duties, and joys of marriage are presented as matters of spiritual significance. From a Christian perspective, marriage must never be seen as a mere human invention—an option for those who choose such a high level of commitment—for it is an arena in which God's glory is displayed in the right ordering of the man and the woman, and their glad reception of all that marriage means, gives, and requires.

Clearly, something has gone badly wrong in our understanding of marriage. This is not only reflected in much of the conversation and literature about marriage found in the secular world, but in many Christian circles as well. The undermining of marriage—or at least its reduction to something less than the biblical concept—is also evident in the way many Christians marry, and in the way others fail to marry.

In the larger culture of confusion, marriage is seen by some persons as an option for those who "need" it. A revolution in the law has made divorce easy and quick, undermining the marital bond and redefining marriage as a tentative commitment. Some of these who desire marriage are driven by the wrong desires. Some are looking for social benefits as others see marriage as a form of self-expression. By any measure, marriage is in trouble.

All this cries out for biblical correction, and Christians must resist the accommodationist temptation to accept the marginalization of marriage. This generation of young Christians must lead the way in the recovery of the biblical vision, and build a Christian counter-culture that puts marriage back at the center of human life and Christian living. This will mean that this generation must recover the glory and gift of marriage as it is presented in Scripture.

In this counter-culture—distinct from the confusions of the age— marriage will be seen as a major life goal and a matter of assuming adulthood. Young Christians will see marriage, not as one "lifestyle" option, but as a means of demonstrating the glory of God in the midst of a fallen world.

Candice Watters clearly shares this vision and offers genuine help to Christians thinking about marriage, adulthood, and God's purpose for humanity. She speaks specifically to young Christian women, offering helpful suggestions about how women can prepare themselves for marriage.

—R. ALBERT MOHLER JR.

The professor's grenade

W*hat? Did he just say what I think he did?*
I was sitting in class learning about all the ways our country was slipping from its constitutional foundations. And in a moment of exasperation, I raised my hand and called out, "So what's the solution?" I really wanted to know, though I'm not sure I believed there was one.

I had just started a graduate program in public policy after having worked on Capitol Hill for two years. I'd seen the new legislators come to Washington with big plans for making a difference. Sometimes they did. But typically, the legislative calendar, seniority, and parliamentary procedure made getting anything done a grindingly slow process. Like turning the *Titanic*. I knew how hard it was to change the culture and was losing my will to believe there really was a solution. But I was hoping that maybe this passionate, articulate, creative professor had some new ideas to teach us. I was tired of losing and worried about the future. I wanted him to have an answer to my question.

Dr. Hubert Morken didn't disappoint. He looked at me with a twinkle in his eye and let his grenade fly: "Get married, make babies, and do government! *That's* how we win."

His response was so different from what I was expecting that it nearly knocked the wind out of me. I always assumed by doing government, I was fighting for the family. But Dr. Morken was suggesting that the very act of forming families was essential to winning.

I was offended. Here I was, pursuing a master's degree so I could go back to Washington and work to defend the rights of traditional families. *I* was the answer to the problem, not them. They already had all the benefits of marriage and family. And now these families were esteemed as the solution to the problem?

"I want to be married," I said. "But that opportunity hasn't come my way. So I've devoted myself to working on behalf of families. I'm doing all this hard work so they can enjoy their cozy life in the suburbs," I said, with not a little envy and bitterness.

Truth is, I wanted nothing more than to be where they were. My life of devoted service on their behalf was a consolation prize. And not a very good one. I suppose some women really do prefer career to family. But I wasn't one of them.

"Candice," he said, almost laughing, "do the math. The people who form families, who raise children and send them into the next generation, are the ones who will influence where our government and culture go in the future."

What he said was politically accurate. The side with the most voters wins. But what he said also made sense spiritually. It was, for me, personally profound.

At this point, the conversation shifted toward some other element of the lecture, but I was transfixed. His "solution" was to me a challenge—a challenge to my whole way of thinking. I always assumed marriage was wonderful if you were lucky enough to get the opportunity; but I was worried that my luck had run out. I really did worry that I was one of those few people who were called to be single. That was the last thing I wanted, but the sheer dread of extended celibacy did little to lessen my fear that God would call me to it anyway.

Even though I grew up in a Christian home, with parents who were committed to staying married, and even though I was a big fan of babies—there were five of us kids—I had picked up the idea from the Christian culture around me that celibate service was superior to marriage and that to be truly spiritual, you had to at least be open to the possibility. Now this professor was telling me that God's plan for believers, most of them anyway, and for the future good of society, was marriage and babies. Family. It was a shock to my system.

If what the professor was saying was just his opinion, I could stay offended. But what if his statement pointed to something deeper? Even though I was going for another degree, even though my outward appearance was all business, what I really wanted, more than anything, was to be a wife and mom. I knew there was an element of pragmatism in his conclusion. But there was something much deeper—something supernatural. This was a class about biblical principles of government, and the professor of the class was a devout believer. Dr. Morken was hinting at what he believed about God's design, God's will. And that design was marriage. If it was still God's will for most people, maybe God would help me get there.

If what Dr. Morken was saying was true, if he was the messenger, a divine mouthpiece, then I had every reason to hope for, and even work for, marriage. And once that idea took hold, I felt free to hope for the first time in over ten years. Not since I was a giddy teenager poring over bridal magazines had I been this excited about marriage. My marriage. For the first time in my adult life, I believed it could—and should—happen.

The Professor's Wife

Mary Morken was the wife of the grenade-throwing professor. She had quite a reputation for matching couples—over thirty to date. And she talked about marriage in a way I'd never heard before. Despite all the positive marriage influences in my upbringing, I still had a lot to learn.

My education began at a retreat center in Virginia. After we nearly begged them out of matchmaking retirement, Hubert and Mary agreed to speak to the students in our class about their story. As we gathered around the stone fireplace, Mary told about how she and Hubert had been at Wheaton together many years before. They were close friends in a prayer group in college but never with a hint of romance. It wasn't until just after graduation that Hubert realized for the first time that Mary was someone special. He said it was as if, in his mind's eye, the word *wife* suddenly flashed across her forehead. He thought, *She'd make a great wife for someone—why not me?*

Mary admitted she'd been in love with Hubert all along, but never let on. She prayed God would open his eyes and worked at being the best friend to him she could be. Listening to her speak, I couldn't help but notice the similarities between her story and mine. I had recently started hanging out with a fellow classmate, and though we were becoming good friends, I wanted it to be more. I was desperate for more information and advice.

After they finished, they took questions. Mary talked about why the times we live in make it so hard for marriages to form. "The culture we live in is anti-marriage," she said. "So many of the customs and unwritten social rules that once helped to naturally bring young men and women together now seem to pull them apart."

She talked differently about marriage than what I was used to. She said marriage was good. She said God created it for our benefit and that He still wants Christians to marry and have families. But she didn't stop there. "Be open about your desire to marry," she said. "Talk about it with your friends, just like you talk about all the other things you hope to do." She even went so far as to say, "In our anti-marriage culture you have to be strategic."

The men my girlfriends and I knew were passive in the midst of a relationally chaotic society. So being passive in return was getting us nowhere. But I was confused. Wasn't it my role as a Christian woman to just wait? "To be feminine is to *nurture*, not merely *respond*," Mary said. "Women have the advantage when it comes to verbal skills, and they can bring healing to the very men they need to take more initiative."

A light went off in my head—I hadn't realized what I was up against. Up till then, I thought just praying for a husband was enough. I thought being spiritually prepared was the full extent of what I could do toward getting married. But here she was saying there was an active role I could play to help it happen. I was ready to accept that challenge. And it made all the difference. With the help of the professor's wife, I started to figure out how to get to marriage. I needed her fresh vision to overcome the hurdles set up by our culture And I needed to understand the dimensions—and limitations—of what I could do.

FINDING THE BEST PATH

You may have a hunch it's not as easy to get married as it once was. If so, you're right. Since 1970, the marriage rate has declined 50 percent.[1] In that time, the proportion of American women ages 25–29 who have not married has quadrupled.[2] Currently the average age of first marriages is 26 for women, 27 for men—as old as it's ever been.[3] Conventional wisdom says later marriage means the bride and groom will be more prepared for the responsibilities of marriage, but many women are ready now. And they're frustrated by the delay. Sociologists blame the delay on the additional educational and career development necessary to marry well.[4] Add to that the confusion over gender roles, cultural worship of youth, the lack of biblical literacy, uninvolved parents and extended family, the fallout from divorce, disengaged social circles, and an often-silent church; and you have the makings for much uncertainty.[5] Women are left wondering, what's the best path to marriage?

The Morkens helped me answer that question. But their wisdom—in the classroom and on that retreat—wasn't just meant for a small group of students. It applies to every Christian single who longs for marriage. If in the midst of these cultural realities, "just pray and wait" sentiments leave you depressed, I think you'll be encouraged by the message of this book: there's something you can do.

Whether you're wondering if you'll ever get a date, stuck in a "just-friends" relationship, or worried that the guy you've been seeing forever will never move toward marriage, this book offers help. It's for all the women who long for marriage but are afraid to admit it, embarrassed by their deepest desires, or concerned that maybe they want it too much. It's for the parents of single women who wonder if there's anything they can do. And it's for married friends of singles who want to help but don't want to intrude.

This is not another book about seeking fulfillment in your singleness. As beings created in God's image, we were designed for relationship—that's why extended singleness leaves so many women discontent. It's also why we should be intentional about finding fulfillment in marriage. Getting married isn't just something that's "nice if it happens." Marriage is what most of us are called to pursue.

I'm not advocating getting married at all costs. But marrying well, for God's glory, is a worthy pursuit. There's a difference between *making* it happen and *helping* it happen. I'm not going to parrot the "girl-power" feminist worldview. Men have a key role to play. And how the single women they know relate to them has everything to do with their momentum toward marriage. This isn't a book about desperation or the hyperactivity of joining every dating service and singles group. You won't find a list of a hundred tips for meeting a hot man or five things you can do today to help you get married tomorrow.

What you will find is a way to *live like you're planning to marry*. Not just having a hope chest—but cultivating a lifestyle that is consistent with the season of marriage ahead. A life that's in harmony with God's work on your behalf; a life that nurtures men and the community around you to play their roles so that you don't have to carry it all. Finally, you'll find in the context of this marriage-minded lifestyle a new confidence to pray like you never have—trusting that marriage is a goal within your grasp. You can risk hoping that you will get married. You really can help it happen.

*Marriage was ordained for a remedy
and to increase the world and for the man
to help the woman and the woman the man,
with all love and kindness.*

WILLIAM TYNDALE

CHAPTER 1

Believe marriage is a worthwhile and holy pursuit

Marriage won't meet all your needs."

"Marriage won't give you all the answers."

"Marriage won't fill the emptiness."

"You can only find fulfillment in God."

Every one of these statements is true. But they're missing something: they're missing the context of Adam's problem.

If it's true that God is all we need for fulfillment, then no one was in a better position to be fully satisfied than Adam. Until Jesus came into the world, no other human had closer and more intimate fellowship with God than Adam. He was in a prime position to find all the answers, to fill all the emptiness, and to have all his needs met in unbroken relationship with the Creator of the universe.

Still God looked down on Adam and said something out of synch with everything else He had said about His creation. At the end of each day of creation, "God saw that it was good." But about Adam,

God said, "It is not good." What wasn't good? Genesis 2:18a tells us, "The Lord God said, 'It is not good for the man to be alone.' "

What did God meant by "not good"? Del Tackett, president of the Focus on the Family Institute, explains it wasn't a qualitative statement—as if God created a three-legged dog and said, "This is not good." He says it was an ethical statement of badness, as in "man *should not* be alone."[1] Why was it *not good* for man to be alone? Because Adam was created in God's image. He was made to reflect God in every aspect of his existence. From all eternity God was in perfect relationship within the Trinity as Father, Son, and Holy Spirit. For Adam to accurately reflect being made in the image of God, he could not remain alone; he had to be in relationship. Adam alone contradicted God's nature.

And so God said, "I will make a helper suitable for him." The story continues. "So the Lord God caused the man to fall into a deep sleep; and while he was sleeping, he took one of the man's ribs and closed up the place with flesh. Then the Lord God made a singles group, and He brought it to the man to alleviate his loneliness."

Of course that's not what the text says. Why is it then that I so often hear this Scripture used to explain our need for just about every kind of relational structure except marriage? While it's true that God goes on to create other social structures to meet certain human needs (such as civil government and the church), He started with marriage. His specific and immediate solution for Adam's problem was a wife. Genesis says,

※※※※

Then the Lord God made a woman from the rib
he had taken out of the man, and he brought her
to the man. The man said, "This is now bone of
my bones and flesh of my flesh; she shall be called
'woman,' for she was taken out of man." For this reason

get married

a man will leave his father and mother and be united to his
wife, and they will become one flesh. The man and his wife
were both naked, and they felt no shame.

(Genesis 2:22–25)

One of the best explanations I've seen on this passage comes
from *The Wycliffe Bible Commentary*:

The inspired author indirectly reveals man's natural
loneliness and lack of full satisfaction. Though much had
been done for him, yet he was conscious of a lack. The
Creator had not finished. He had plans for providing a
companion who would satisfy the unfulfilled yearnings of
man's heart. Created for fellowship and companionship,
man could enter into the full life only as he might share
love, trust, and devotion in the intimate circle of the
family relationship. Jehovah made it possible for man to
have "an help meet for him." Literally, *a help answering
to him*, or, *one who answers*. She was to be one who could
share man's responsibilities, respond to his nature with
understanding and love, and wholeheartedly co-operate
with him in working out the plan of God.[2]

THE ONGOING CREATION MANDATE

Only after God created male and female does Genesis
say, "God saw all that He had made, and behold, it was very
good." And to Adam and Eve jointly, God gives the marching
orders for mankind: "God blessed them; and God said to them,
'Be fruitful and multiply, and fill the earth, and subdue it; and rule
over the fish of the sea and over the birds of the sky and over every
living thing that moves on the earth' " (v. 28 NASB).

believe marriage is a worthwhile and holy pursuit   23

It wasn't just for companionship that Adam needed Eve. God had work for them to do. And for this work, Adam needed a helpmate. In a marriage that made them "one flesh," Eve complemented Adam's abilities and made it possible for the two of them to be fruitful, to subdue the earth, and to take dominion. Theologians call this the "creation mandate." Dr. Morkin explained that within the command for fruitfulness and dominion is the framework for everything we are called to do in our work and families. When challenged that this was only God's way of "jump-starting" the world, Dr. Morken answered boldly, "The creation mandate has never been rescinded. Never in Scripture did God say, 'OK, I have enough people now. You can stop getting married and having babies.' "

God continues to call His people to this work in order to accomplish His purposes. In Isaiah 45, the prophet reinforces the creation mandate, writing,

Woe to him who says to his father, "What have you begotten?" or to his mother, "What have you brought to birth?" This is what the Lord says—the Holy One of Israel, and its Maker: Concerning things to come, do you question me about my children, or give me orders about the work of my hands? It is I who made the earth and created mankind upon it. My own hands stretched out the heavens; I marshaled their starry hosts. For this is what the Lord says—He who created the heavens, he is God; he who fashioned and made the earth, he founded it; he did not create it to be empty, but formed it to be inhabited—he says: "I am the Lord, and there is no other."

(ISAIAH 45:10–12, 18)

get married

"But didn't Jesus change everything?" some ask. The redemptive work of Christ did change our perspective on much of the Old Testament, but it didn't negate the first thirty-nine books of the Bible. Jesus said, "Do not think that I have come to abolish the Law or the Prophets; I have not come to abolish them but to fulfill them" (Matthew 5:17).

"Christ's atoning work at Calvary was not, and was not intended to be, God's provision for the needs that marriage meets," writes Ellen Varughese in *The Freedom to Marry*. "Whether in a state of sin or in a state of righteousness, whether under law or under grace, man still needs marriage."[3]

A GIFT OF COMMON GRACE

Even if a couple doesn't acknowledge Jesus as Lord and Savior, even if they're not aware of the creation mandate, they can still partake of the goodness of marriage. Even in a day when women don't *need* marriage for the same practical reasons they once did, social research reinforces the truth that God created marriage for our good. One of the best collections of evidence is *The Case for Marriage* by Linda Waite and Maggie Gallagher. What they and others have discovered in the natural realm reinforces the timeless wisdom found in Scripture:

Ecclesiastes 4:9 says, "Two are better than one, because they have a good return for their work."

Waite and Gallagher say, "The old adage 'Two can live as cheaply as one' contains more than a grain of truth. Husbands and wives usually need only one set of furniture and appliances, one set of dishes, one lawn mower. . . . This kind of pooling means couples can have the same standard of living for much less money or effort than can an adult living alone."[4]

Proverbs 18:22 says, "He who finds a wife finds what is good and receives favor from the Lord."

Steven L. Nock says, "Masculinity is precarious and must be sustained in adulthood. Normative marriage does this. A man develops, sustains, and displays his masculine identity in his marriage. The adult roles that men occupy as husbands are core aspects of their masculinity."[5]

Matthew 19:6 says, "So they are no longer two, but one. Therefore what God has joined together, let man not separate."

Waite and Gallagher again: "The promise of permanence is key to marriage's transformative power. People who expect to be part of a couple for their entire lives—unless something awful happens—organize their lives differently from people who are less certain their relationship will last. The marriage contract, because it is long-term, encourages husbands and wives to make decisions jointly and to function as part of a team. Each spouse expects to be able to count on the other to be there and to fulfill his or her responsibilities."[6]

Song of Songs 1:2 says, "Let him kiss me with the kisses of his mouth—for your love is more delightful than wine."

Waite and Gallagher say, "Married people have both more and better sex than singles do. They not only have sex more often, but they enjoy it more, both physically and emotionally, than do their unmarried counterparts. Only cohabitors have more sex than married couples, but they don't necessarily enjoy it as much. Marriage, it turns out, is not only good for you, it is good for your libido too."[7]

The goodness of marriage comes when we surrender to the timeless institution that was endowed with meaning and purpose before we were ever born. I was pleasantly surprised that one popular writer called her book *Surrendering to Marriage*. What could be more countercultural than "surrendering" to marriage in a day when more and more people are bringing contemporary consumer values to everything? As rugged individualists, we are what some have called "prosumers," and we like to put our stamp on everything, to re-create things in our own image. Couples today write their own vows, keep separate banking accounts, and more in their effort to individualize and personalize their marriage. But marriage doesn't gain value by the meaning we try to bring to it. Our attempts to reshape it or improve it undermine the blessings God designed to flow from the created version—blessings not only for us as couples, but for the children of faithful marriages, for the communities they undergird, and for generations to come.

RICHER BLESSINGS IN CHRIST

The richest benefits of marriage appear when couples submit to the sacrificial design of Christian marriage (Ephesians 5:22–31), and stick with it even when they don't see immediate benefits. This is especially true when it means staying faithful to their vows when they are on the less pleasurable side of "for better or worse, for richer or poorer, in sickness and in health." The best things about marriage are the things born out of sacrifice, commitment, and crucible. St. Francis de Sales said it this way: "The state of marriage is one that requires more virtue and constancy than any other. It is a perpetual exercise of mortification. . . . From this thyme plant, in spite of the bitter nature of its juice, you may be able to draw and make the honey of a holy life."[8]

Even as couples embrace the blessings, marriage is bigger than any one couple. Ultimately, like everything else in our lives, it's an opportunity to give God glory. Malachi 2:15 says, "Has not the Lord made them one? In flesh and spirit they are his. And why one? Because he was seeking godly offspring. So guard yourself in your spirit, and do not break faith with the wife of your youth."

In addition to using marriage as the means for "godly offspring," God also holds out the union between man and woman as a reflection of His relationship with His people.

Isaiah 54:5 says, "For your Maker is your husband—the Lord Almighty is his name—the Holy One of Israel is your Redeemer; he is called the God of all the earth." The apostle Paul showed the significance of how each couple reflects God's marriage relationship with His people when he wrote: " 'For this reason a man will leave his father and mother and be united to his wife, and the two will become one flesh.' This is a profound mystery— but I am talking about Christ and the church. However, each one of you also must love his wife as he loves himself, and the wife must respect her husband" (Ephesians 5:31–32).

This Scripture reminds us that God created marriage for our good, and also for His higher purposes—it's ultimately about Him.

Knowing God made marriage for our good and His glory isn't always enough. Many singles overspiritualize their single state, thinking it's more holy to look only to God for fulfillment. But that's inconsistent with how He made us. Dominic Aquila, president of New Geneva Seminary, says, "We know that our physical food and drink cannot ultimately meet needs provided by the bread of life and by living water. However, we don't look at a meal spread before us and say, 'No thanks, God is all I need.' That's why a gift is needed so that celibates can have needs met that are otherwise met by Biblical marriage."[9]

Like good food satisfies an empty belly, for most believers, good marriages satisfy loneliness and other core needs. God's command to be fruitful and multiply and take dominion of the earth persists. The work He called us to is not yet complete. The assignments of the garden still stand. And marriage is central to that work. Unless your calling would be inhibited by marriage and family, and you're especially gifted to surrender marriage and all its benefits for lifelong celibacy, marriage is still normative and the appropriate channel for your God-given desires for companionship, sexual intimacy, and the partnership essential for completing your life's work while bringing God glory.

get married

*E*STEEMING MARRIAGE ALONGSIDE CELIBACY

If marriage is essential to meeting our needs and central to what we are called to do in life, why does the New Testament seem to talk more about singleness? In Matthew 22:30, Jesus says, "At the resurrection people will neither marry nor be given in marriage; they will be like the angels in heaven."

Does this suggest God is shifting gears from His original plan for marriage toward singleness? Why won't human marriage exist in heaven? Hear what Scripture has to say:

Then I heard what sounded like a great multitude,
like the roar of rushing waters and like loud peals of thunder,
shouting: "Hallelujah! For our Lord God Almighty reigns.
Let us rejoice and be glad and give him glory! For the wedding
of the Lamb has come, and his bride has made herself ready.
Fine linen, bright and clean, was given her to wear."
(Fine linen stands for the righteous acts of the saints.)
Then the angel said to me, "Write: 'Blessed are those who
are invited to the wedding supper of the Lamb!'"

(REVELATION 19:6–9)

We will all be "single" in heaven so that we can become the bride of Christ, so that we can experience the perfect marriage. Marriage is the norm, both now *and* in the age to come. It's only the nature of the bridegroom that will change. In heaven, we'll turn our attention to Christ, the Bridegroom all human husbands foretell. Every marriage since Adam and Eve's has pointed to the ultimate wedding between Christ and His church (that's why it matters how we go about being husbands and wives). Heaven won't mark the end of marriage, but its culmination.

FRUITFUL WITHOUT FAMILY

Why then did Jesus commend those who "renounced marriage because of the kingdom"? Jesus had just explained to the Pharisees that God's standard for marital conduct exceeded what the law required. His disciples responded stating, "If this is the situation between a husband and wife, it is better not to marry" (Matthew 19:10). Jesus answered them, "Not everyone can accept this word, but only those to whom it has been given. For some are eunuchs because they were born that way; others were made that way by men; and others have renounced marriage because of the kingdom of heaven. The one who can accept this should accept it" (Matthew 19:12).

Jesus didn't come to do away with marriage; what He said to the Pharisees confirms that. But His words about eunuchs do show a new place for those who were once considered unfruitful. In the Old Testament, marriage and children were so essential to life and God's purposes that not experiencing them was a great sorrow that also put people at a significant economic and social disadvantage. Growing a godly nation made the work of family an essential element of living out their commitment to Yahweh. Thanks to their faithfulness in marriage and parenting, the lineage continued, connecting the promises of old with the Messiah. His arrival ushered in a new kingdom where even those who didn't marry or have natural children were still capable of playing a significant role as God's hands and feet in a needy world.

In the midst of the new opportunities for kingdom work, as well as the challenges of persecution faced by the early church, believers started asking some tough questions: Where does marriage fit in to this new kingdom? What about sex? Is it OK to just serve God in our singleness, or do we need to get married?

Many of these questions came from the church in Corinth. Located in southern Greece, Corinth was a challenging place for new Christians. Its pagan culture embraced sex outside of marriage, homosexuality, and polygamy. In the midst of this relational chaos, some Corinthian Christians—even some who were already married—wondered if it would be better for them to be single and to abstain from sex. Paul answered their questions about sex and marriage in what we now know as 1 Corinthians 7. This passage gives the most detail anywhere in the Bible about the possibility of dedicated celibate service. It's clear Paul sees great potential for service among those who are willing to be celibate on behalf of the kingdom, especially in light of what he referred to as "the present distress" (7:26 NASB).

THE MARRIAGE IMPERATIVE

What's often ignored in our day is how much in this same passage Paul also esteemed marriage. Not only that, but he held it up as an imperative for any believer lacking self-control. "Let them marry," he said, "for it is better to marry than to burn with passion." He had already told his married audience that it wasn't more pious to abstain from marital sex in order to serve God—that, in fact, they shouldn't deprive one another (1 Corinthians 7:3–5 NASB). Now he was telling never-marrieds that staying that way for the kingdom wasn't more pious if it meant they were prone to sexual sin.

The Greek tense for "let them marry," says John MacArthur, is a command, a strong imperative "since a person can't live a happy life and serve the Lord effectively if dominated by unfulfilled sexual passion."[10] This reinforces Paul's earlier point in which he follows his statement, "It is good for a man not to marry," with "but since there is so much immorality, each man should have his own wife, and each woman her own husband" (vv.1–2).

Paul repeatedly warned believers, in 1 Corinthians 6:9–20; Ephesians 5:3; Colossians 3:5; and 1 Thessalonians 4:3–4, about the temptations of sexual sin. In the midst of describing the possibilities of single service, he reiterated his concern about sexual sin, stressing that marriage is the *only* acceptable path for sexual fulfillment. "Marriage is such an important part of honoring God as sexual beings," said Mary Morken. "I don't know how people can make it morally without getting married. I've met very few who have." Research supports her experience. With the rate of premarital sex among Christians mirroring that of unbelievers—77 percent of men raised in "Fundamentalist Protestant homes" admit to premarital sex[11]—it's clear that Paul's admonition to marry is as relevant as ever.

Only after he addressed the problem of sexual sin did Paul discuss the potential for spiritual devotion in celibacy. He wrote, "The woman who is unmarried, and the virgin, is concerned about the things of the Lord, that she may be holy both in body and spirit; but one who is married is concerned about the things of the world, how she may please her husband" (1 Corinthians 7:34 NASB). John MacArthur's commentary about this verse says, "Marriage does not prevent great devotion to the Lord, but it brings more potential matters to interfere with it. . . . Singleness has fewer hindrances," he says, "though not guaranteed greater spiritual virtue."[12] While married people are concerned with pleasing each other, those who are not married still face other distractions in their attempt to be fully devoted to the Lord.

Jesus explained it this way: In the parable of the soils He said, "Still others, like seed sown among thorns, hear the word; but the worries of this life, the deceitfulness of wealth and the desires for other things come in and choke the word, making it unfruitful" (Mark 4:18–19). Paul knew this teaching and reaffirmed often how the cares of this world can rob us of our devotion to God (Romans 12:2, Colossians 2:8).

After telling the Corinthians that someone who is unmarried can have "undistracted devotion to the Lord" (1 Corinthians 7:35 NASB), he clarified in a letter to Timothy that unmarried women are vulnerable to idleness. He warned that young widows pledging themselves to celibate service may later find themselves wanting to break that pledge because of their sensual desires. "They get into the habit of being idle and going about from house to house. And not only do they become idlers, but also gossips and busybodies, saying things they ought not to. So, I counsel younger widows to marry, to have children, to manage their homes and to give the enemy no opportunity for slander" (1 Timothy 5:13–14).

Paul explained to the Corinthians that a married woman is concerned with how to take care of her husband (a statement of fact, not a criticism). But he didn't stop there. His letter to Timothy showed he also believed that the responsibilities of marriage are honorable and an antidote to idleness. This is consistent with the Proverbs 31 description of a wife of noble character who, "watches over the affairs of her household and does not eat the bread of idleness" (Proverbs 31:27).

Surveying the overarching themes of Paul's writings, it's clear that he believed an unmarried woman has the potential to serve the kingdom in a greater way, but if she is not gifted to overcome her vulnerability to sexual temptation and idleness, it is better for her to marry and serve God in marriage.

If you believe you can forgo marriage and its benefits—sex, children, companionship—and be fully expended in serving the Lord, you likely have the gift of celibacy, and many blessings would confer on you for living the life of selfless service to God. If, however, you frequently notice your sex drive and find it makes you vulnerable to temptation, and if you find it difficult to avoid idleness in order to have what Paul calls "undistracted devotion to the Lord," then you're called to marry. Marriage is not a compromise. It is not a spiritually inferior path. It's what God is calling you to for your good and His glory.

CELIBATE SERVANT OR SIMPLY SINGLE?

If you're going on a missions trip once a year, volunteering at church twice a week, and holding down a traditional job, and on top of it all, dating the cute new guy in your singles group, you're not following the celibate service job description. Just because you're single doesn't mean you have the gift Paul described, or the desire and capacity for the lifestyle that gift makes possible. In our culture, a single woman must take pains to experience "undistracted devotion to the Lord." There are few, if any, cultural expectations placed upon her that require selfless service.

When I was single I had lots of discretionary time, even with a demanding job. I could have devoted hours to charity work. I could have spent it at church, or building homes, or ladling soup. But the truth is, I gave in to the temptation to spend it at a tiny table at Borders sipping iced hazelnut lattes, reading books ,and writing in my journal. I'm not saying it's a sin to do that, but it wasn't the stuff of "undistracted devotion."

I wasn't even doing as much in His service as my married friends were. Sadly, that's not unusual. While there are some first-class single Christians serving faithfully, most Christian singles spend their free time doing things outside the realm of biblically defined celibate service. While 29 percent of married people told Barna Research that they had volunteered to help a church in the past seven days, only 14 percent of never-married people had.[13] The time today's singles have available for spiritual service is the same time the leisure and entertainment industry demands from them.

In my experience, the demands of caring for spouse and children have actually pushed me closer to holiness and pulled me further away from the temptations of idleness. I think of just the range of challenges I typically confront before sunrise on any given day—waking up at 5 a.m. with a teething baby, trying to squeeze in some devotional time before the older kids wake up, getting the kids their baths and breakfast, starting the laundry, cleaning up the kitchen, and working on an article with a pressing deadline. Compare that to when I was single. Back then the only person I had to worry about in the morning was me. I was the only one I had to feed, bathe, and clothe. My quiet time was limited only by my own decision to sleep too late, and the biggest obstacle to my goals for the morning was traffic.

Marriage and parenting provide a crucible for holiness unlike any other. I think that's why author Gary Thomas asks, "What if God designed marriage to make us holy more than to make us happy?" [14]

I say all this not to discourage you from longing for marriage and family. The work, though "bone wearying,"[15] produces fruit richer, sweeter, more nourishing than anything I tasted before marriage. I say it to provide a reality check for those who insist staying single is more holy, more useful to the kingdom. I would remind them that for every Mother Teresa and Amy Carmichael, there was a Susanna Wesley, Abigail Adams, and Ruth Bell Graham. And in our culture, it's more likely that for every weary mother, daily sacrificing her own time, energy, and resources for her husband and children, there are singles who are virtually indistinguishable from their unbelieving friends.

The kingdom ushered in by Jesus brought new esteem and opportunities for celibate service, but not a spiritual fig leaf for any and all single lifestyles. When Paul said he wished others could be like him, he didn't just mean his marital status. He meant his undistracted devotion to God.

In his second letter to the Corinthians he gave a glimpse of what that devotion looked like:

We put no stumbling block in anyone's path, so that our ministry will not be discredited. Rather, as servants of God we commend ourselves in every way: in great endurance;

in troubles, hardships and distresses; in beatings,
imprisonments and riots; in hard work, sleepless nights
and hunger; in purity, understanding, patience and kindness;
in the Holy Spirit and in sincere love; in truthful speech and
in the power of God; with weapons of righteousness in the
right hand and in the left; through glory and dishonor,
bad report and good report; genuine, yet regarded as
impostors; known, yet regarded as unknown; dying, and
yet we live on; beaten, and yet not killed; sorrowful, yet
always rejoicing; poor, yet making many rich; having
nothing, and yet possessing everything.

(2 CORINTHIANS 6:3–10)

This is the high calling that often accompanies celibate service. Interestingly, it's the same high calling that patriarchs like Moses, prophets like Isaiah, apostles like Peter, missionaries like Jim Elliot, evangelists like Billy Graham, and scores of other people have followed over the years while also (or maybe because of) taking on the responsibility of marriage and children. Both the call to celibate service and the call to marriage are of high value in God's eyes when they are submitted to His purposes.

We should be honest about our current culture and recognize that the epidemic of sexual immorality and demands of the leisure industry make it very difficult for many singles to be like Paul was. Were that not true, the swelling population of Christian singles in the world today could have already set off a great revival.

To women (and especially men) who aren't prepared to lay their sexuality and time on the altar in order to "secure undistracted devotion to the Lord," Paul says, "each man is to have his own wife, and each woman is to have her own husband" (1 Corinthians 7:35, 2 NASB).

get married

*For everything created by God
is good, and nothing is to be rejected if it
is received with gratitude for it is sanctified
by means of the word of God and prayer.*

1 TIMOTHY 4:1-5 NASB

CHAPTER 2

Restore biblical
honor and desire

Scripture leaves no doubt that marriage remains the high and holy calling for most believers. Why, then, are women—even those who desire it—having such a hard time getting married? Could it be that discouragement and distraction are a big part of why so many single women are thwarted in their goal of marriage? I believe a woman's attitude has everything to do with her ability to marry well.

I've never been a hard-core athlete. Soft-core is more accurate—a three-mile run is my personal best, and the last time I played team sports was in junior high. But this much I do know: a competitive athlete's ability to win begins in her mind. (That, and if all those athletic commercials are to be believed, having the right gear and clothes.) Like Yogi Berra said, in the way only he could, "Ninety percent of the game is half mental." No serious athlete would allow her mind to be cluttered with compromising thoughts about the sport she's competing in.

How could she stay focused if she spent all her time with friends who made fun of her event and the goals she was trying to achieve? How much would it benefit her to listen to people who crashed and burned in her sport and relished warning others to not even try?

What if that same need for focus applies to our thoughts about marriage?

What marriage messages are you absorbing? What are you learning from TV and movies? What do you hear from the women around you? The greatest criticism of marriage often flows from those who have been hurt the most: abandoned wives and their children. But it's no longer limited to those who've suffered through divorce. These days, dishonor flows from every direction: books for singles; university lecture halls; tabloid headlines; and sitcoms about overweight, lazy, dim-witted husbands and their gorgeous, super-smart, belittling wives. Yet Hebrews 13:4 says, "Marriage is to be held in honor among all" (NASB).

When you're frustrated in your efforts to marry, it's tempting to build singleness up and tear marriage down. I've seen lots of examples of writers who say they want to be married in one breath and, with the next, say they're glad to learn that marriage isn't all it's cracked up to be. They remind me of Aesop's fox. As the story goes,

"One hot summer day a Fox was strolling through an orchard. He saw a bunch of Grapes ripening high on a grapevine. 'Just the thing to quench my thirst,' he said. Backing up a few paces, he took a run and jumped at the Grapes, just missing. Turning around again, he ran faster and jumped again. Still a miss. Again and again he jumped, until at last he gave up out of exhaustion. Walking away with his nose in the air, he said: 'I am sure they are sour.' "[1]

So common is the trend among singles to knock marriage that I wonder if they even realize they're doing it. I know I didn't. When I was single I assumed I was honoring marriage. *After all*, I reasoned, *how could I dishonor something I wanted so badly?* The truth is, it's not that hard. Especially in our culture, where conventional wisdom says it's the unmarried—both single and divorced—who have all the fun. But Scripture is clear: marriage as God created it is to be held in high esteem.

IT'S NOT FUNNY

Early in my conversations with the Morkens, they mentioned their long-standing commitment to Ephesians 5:4: "Nor should there be obscenity, foolish talk or coarse joking, which are out of place, but rather thanksgiving." They resolved to never joke about marriage, sex, or divorce. I thought that was a pretty obvious standard for Christians to uphold. Obvious, but not easy. Until then, I hadn't realized just how ubiquitous that kind of joking was. Of course, it was all over television, but it was pretty common among my Christian friends too. Trying to challenge it when I heard it among my peers was tough. It reminded me of all the times growing up when I had to ask my friends to choose a different movie because I wasn't allowed to watch the one they wanted to see.

It's hard to take a stand on this issue all by yourself—the first time I did it was with Steve Watters. I think he was more offended by my challenge to the propriety of his humor than I was offended by his joke. But we worked through it and set a precedent for our relationship that it was OK to bring up difficult subjects in order to resolve them. We also agreed that together we would support marriage and purity and discourage joking about it whenever we heard it. That produced some benefits we didn't anticipate. Among my friends, the less we joked about marriage or sex, the more seriously we took it—a major change of perspective that led to a positive change in behavior among both women and men. I think that's part of why God wants us to honor marriage. It's not just a blind command to never disrespect what He designed. He knows that dishonor will disappoint our efforts to marry well.

OUR ROLE MODELS

The Bible doesn't just tell us to honor marriage; it shows us how. Jesus, John the Baptist, Paul, and Jeremiah all served the kingdom in their singleness, but they also showed by their words and actions tremendous honor and esteem for marriage.

JEREMIAH

Though Jeremiah never married, it wasn't for any reason of personal preference or disdain for the institution. As far as we know, he is the only person in the Bible who received a direct word from God saying, "Don't get married."

Then the word of the Lord came to me:
"You must not marry and have sons or daughters
in this place." For this is what the Lord says about
the sons and daughters born in this land and about the
women who are their mothers and the men who are
their fathers: "They will die of deadly diseases.
They will not be mourned or buried but will be like
refuse lying on the ground. They will perish by sword
and famine, and their dead bodies will become food
for the birds of the air and the beasts of the earth."

(JEREMIAH 16:1–4)

The realities of warfare and siege were such that marriage in Jeremiah's circumstances would have been a grievous hardship. Still, knowing that didn't necessarily lessen his sense of loss. It wasn't that marriage was suddenly undesirable, but that it was precluded by extraordinary circumstances. Given Jeremiah's environment, God's call could be seen as merciful. It's unlikely his single state was something he aspired to. Jeremiah sacrificed marriage in obedience, but in his culture, it was a sacrifice nonetheless. Given that, it's noteworthy that Jeremiah never went negative on marriage. He esteemed marriage in his inspired writings, upholding it as a reflection of God's covenant relationship with His people. He wrote: " 'Return, faithless people,' declares the Lord, 'for I am your husband. I will choose you—one from a town and two from a clan—and bring you to Zion' " (Jeremiah 3:14; see also Jeremiah 3:1–3; 3:20; 31:32).

JOHN THE BAPTIST

Though John the Baptist never married, he gave his life defending the institution. Herod was a ruthless king who dominated his subjects with intimidation and fear. Unaccustomed to being confronted, he raged when John defied his right to take his brother's wife for his own. John challenged him boldly, saying, "It is not lawful for you to have her." It's hard to imagine such a blatant, or chastening, challenge to a politician's marital infidelity in today's climate of promiscuity. But in John's day, it was scandalous. John's stand landed him in prison and ended up costing him his life (see Matthew 14:1–10).

JESUS

The ultimate example—Jesus, our soon and coming Bridegroom—honored marriage by laying down His life to ransom His unfaithful bride. After He rose from the dead, He promised to "go and prepare a place" (John 14:2–4) for us, the church, where we can be received as His bride (Revelation 19:6–9). Not only did He foreshadow the union He would have with the church for eternity, He raised the standard for human marriages back to God's original design. Just before He introduced the possibility of kingdom service by eunuchs (discussed earlier), He answered the Pharisees' challenge to marriage saying,

"Haven't you read . . . that at the beginning
the Creator 'made them male and female,'
and said, 'For this reason a man will leave
his father and mother and be united to his wife,
and the two will become one flesh'? So they
are no longer two, but one. Therefore what
God has joined together, let man not separate."
"Why then," they [the Pharisees] asked, "did
Moses command that a man give his wife a
certificate of divorce and send her away?"
Jesus replied, "Moses permitted you to
divorce your wives because your hearts
were hard. But it was not this way from
the beginning. I tell you that anyone who
divorces his wife, except for marital unfaithfulness,
and marries another woman commits adultery."

(MATTHEW 19:4 –9)

PAUL

Paul was likely, at one time, married. He may have been a widower when he wrote his letter to the Corinthians—the one that says in effect, "I wish you were as I am," meaning unmarried, or no longer married. Formerly of the Sanhedrin, Paul would have had to be married—it was a requirement of membership. And even though at the writing of 1 Corinthians he no longer was, he still honored the institution alongside his comments about celibate service. Though he chose to stay single for the kingdom, he defended his option to marry, should he want to, asking, "Don't we have the right to take a believing wife along with us, as do the other apostles and the Lord's brothers and Cephas?" (1 Corinthians 9:5).

In his letter to the Ephesians, Paul penned a model for marriage that has stood the test of time. More important, Ephesians 5 goes on to elevate marriage beyond mere husband and wife to a mystery reflecting Christ's relationship with the church.

It's easy to apply our contemporary ideas about singleness to Jeremiah, John the Baptist, Paul, and even Jesus. But their lives were dramatically different from most modern singles— especially in the way they honored marriage in their words and actions. They demonstrated that neither currently single people nor those called to celibate service have reason to be critical of marriage.

MAKING THE IMPOSSIBLE POSSIBLE

We're not limited to biblical examples. Mother Teresa of Calcutta served God in her singleness and also honored marriage. She said, "It is one of those beautiful gifts of God for a young man to love a young woman and a young woman to love a young man. It is a most beautiful gift of God. But make sure that you love each other with a clean heart and that on the day of your marriage you can give each other a virgin heart, a virgin love."[2]

Nowhere in Scripture or the lives of heroic singles like Mother Teresa do we see a pattern of demeaning marriage to make singles feel better about their marital status. And yet that's exactly what so many well-meaning *married* Christians do in our culture. They try to "encourage" the young women they know by saying, "It's better to be single and wish you were married, than to be married and wish you were single," or other similar quips. But that's not a fair comparison—it equates married people on bad days with singles on their best. People who marry well and are committed to their marriages don't wish they were single again, and singles who are honest about their desires don't find consolation in married people having bad days. Most admit marriage is still something they intensely want.

It's difficult to move toward marriage if you're surrounded by messages that dishonor it. And if you entertain and contribute to those messages, it's less likely you'll attract a marriage-minded guy. What's the alternative? Esteeming marriage—not pretending every marriage is perfect, but believing that God's plan for marriage is worthy of honor. That includes spending time with healthy married couples and other singles who honor marriage, and avoiding media that dishonors it, including anything that glorifies divorce or sex outside of marriage.

Aesop's fox is an archetype. It *is* easy to despise what you can't get, even when it's what you want most of all. But that's exactly why you must strain hard against the temptation. Because with marriage, it's nearly impossible to get what you dishonor.

MARRIAGE AS AN IDOL

Most single women want to get married.[3] A good marriage is something they deeply desire. But for many, their desire is unarticulated, a silent longing. I kept quiet most of the time when I was single and hoping for marriage, mostly out of embarrassment for being romantically unsuccessful. It was easier, and less risky, to just keep it to myself. By my silence, I could avoid ridicule and the possibility of having to admit my failure if marriage never happened.

But today there's an added reason women hide their desire for marriage. They've been told and retold that nurturing such a desire will not only scare men off, but worst of all, it may lead them to idolatry. I see and hear this warning a lot among Christians. It seems anytime someone writes or preaches about marriage to singles, they start with the caveat that wanting marriage is good "as long as you don't make an idol out of it."

Can the desire for marriage really become an idol? It's technically possible. But that notion has been blown out of proportion. And repeatedly suggesting the possibility of idolatry has done more harm than good. It's caused a lot of women to be tepid in their approach to marriage and made them afraid that any amount of thinking or acting on their desire might be a sin. Both have the unfortunate consequence of making marriage even less likely to happen.

Such caution is rarely urged with other desires. No one would discourage a woman from praying fervently, even daily, for an unsaved family member. And we'd applaud intense and passionate faith for the healing of a friend who was dying of cancer. Even desires that more easily border on idolatry—education, career pursuits, and hobbies—get a near-universal pass. But giving a fraction of such attention to the desire for marriage solicits dire warnings of overdoing it. Fervency when petitioning God for a mate comes under singular scrutiny.

Idol worship is a serious charge. God's warning against it is the second of the Ten Commandments: "You shall not make for yourself an idol in the form of anything in heaven above or on the earth beneath or in the waters below" (Exodus 20:4). It's also a major liability: "Those who cling to worthless idols forfeit the grace that could be theirs" (Jonah 2:8). How can a Christian woman make sure her desire for marriage doesn't drag her into idolatry?

*W*OOD, STONE, GOLD, AND SEX
For starters, by looking at what the Bible says about it. Almost every one of the more than two hundred idol verses are about objects made of wood, stone, silver, or gold. Physical idols were pervasive at the time the Bible was written and were a direct violation of the second commandment. Considering this overwhelming focus on statues, the first and most obvious thing a woman can do to avoid making marriage an idol is never to bow down to one of those plastic bride and groom miniatures that goes on the top of a wedding cake.

That's easy enough. But what about intangible idols? The prophet Ezekiel said, "Then the word of the Lord came to me: 'Son of man, these men have set up idols in their hearts and put wicked stumbling blocks before their faces . . . ' " (14:2–3). It is possible for us to put other gods before the true God, to worship created things instead of the Creator—even if they can't be seen. "The heart is an idol factory," said John Calvin. But can we really make marriage an idol in our postmarriage culture? Not in the way that's often implied. Where we most often sin in our desire for marriage is not in worshiping marriage itself, but in doubting God's ability to bring it about.

That some would make women doubt the rightness of desiring marriage shouldn't surprise us. Paul told us it would happen. He wrote:

✦✦✦✦✦

But the Spirit explicitly says that in later times
some will fall away from the faith, paying attention
to deceitful spirits and doctrines of demons,
by means of the hypocrisy of liars seared in their
own conscience as with a branding iron,
men who forbid marriage and advocate abstaining
from foods which God has created to be gratefully

shared in by those who believe and know the truth.
For everything created by God is good, and nothing
is to be rejected if it is received with gratitude;
for it is sanctified by means of the word
of God and prayer.

(1 TIMOTHY 4:1–5 NASB)

Sadly, the "marriage as idol" warning prevents many young women from gratefully sharing in what God created as good. And the harder it is to marry well, the more likely it is women will accept cultural counterfeits—premarital sex, endless youth, self-centered singleness—falling into true idolatry of heart. Paul told us what that looks like in Ephesians 5:3–5:

But among you there must not be even a hint
of sexual immorality, or of any kind of impurity,
or of greed, because these are improper for
God's holy people. Nor should there be obscenity,
foolish talk or coarse joking, which are out of place,
but rather thanksgiving. For of this you can be sure:
No immoral, impure or greedy person—such a man
is an idolater—has any inheritance in the
kingdom of Christ and of God.

He repeats this warning again in his letter to the Colossians, "When Christ, who is your life, appears, then you also will appear with him in glory. Put to death, therefore, whatever belongs to your earthly nature: sexual immorality, impurity, lust, evil desires and greed, which is idolatry" (3:4–5).

MacArthur says of these verses, "When people engage in either greed or the sexual sins Paul has catalogued, they follow their desires, rather than God's, in essence worshipping themselves—which is idolatry."[4] That sounds a lot like what James said: "When you ask, you do not receive, because you ask with wrong motives, that you may spend what you get on your pleasures. You adulterous people, don't you know that friendship with the world is hatred toward God?" (4:3–4).

Scripture is clear: idolatry has everything to do with our earthly nature, evil desires, wrong motives, and pursuit of our own pleasures. We're repeatedly told to trust God's ways and resist the ways of the world. David said, "Do not fret because of evil men or be envious of those who do wrong; for like the grass they will soon wither, like green plants they will soon die away" (Psalm 37:1–2).

*T*OO MUCH, OR TOO LITTLE?

These are desires we must avoid—envy, greed, and lust—not the desire for marriage *as God designed it*. Paul said, "But since there is so much immorality, each man should have his own wife, and each woman her own husband" (1 Corinthians 7:2). Not only is it unlikely that a godly woman's desire for a biblical marriage would become an idol, biblical marriage is the antidote to much of the idolatry—"sexual immorality, impurity, lust, evil desires and greed"—that plagues our culture. And it *is* a plague, an epidemic. As such, our desires for biblical marriage, if anything, aren't strong enough.

C. S. Lewis wrote,

Indeed, if we consider the unblushing promises of reward and the staggering nature of the rewards promised in the Gospels, it would seem that Our Lord finds our desires not too strong, but too weak. We are half-hearted creatures, fooling about with drink and sex and ambition when infinite joy is offered us, like an ignorant child who wants to go on making mud pies in a slum because he cannot imagine what is meant by the offer of a holiday at the sea. We are far too easily pleased.[5]

To those whose desires have been manipulated by the Enemy, we could say, "You're fooling about with premarital sex, recreational companions, endless buddies, when what I'm offering you is marriage, the desire of your heart." "Marriage," writes Lewis, "is the proper reward for the real lover, and he is not mercenary for desiring it."[6]

What, then, is the proper channel for our desire for marriage? David advised, "Trust in the Lord and do good; dwell in the land and enjoy safe pasture. Delight yourself in the Lord and he will give you the desires of your heart. Commit your way to the Lord; trust in him and he will do this: he will make your righteousness shine like the dawn, the justice of your cause like the noonday sun" (Psalm 37:3–6).

A genuine posture of delighting in the Lord actually helps us grow in our understanding of what He created marriage to be, replacing our perceptions with His design. It sanctifies our natural desires for it. As Romans 8:5 says, "Those who live according to the sinful nature have their minds set on what that nature desires; but those who live in accordance with the Spirit have their minds set on what the Spirit desires."

With the sacrifice, commitment, and obedience God built into biblical marriage (see Ephesians 5 for details), it continually puts God and His ways above all. A woman who is delighting herself in the Lord, daily committing her ways to Him in prayer, and doing everything unto the glory of God, can trust that her desire for marriage is good and that God is able to grant her desire for the thing He created. She can join the psalmist and say with confidence,

Praise the Lord, O my soul; all my inmost being,
praise his holy name. Praise the Lord, O my soul,
and forget not all his benefits—who forgives all your sins
and heals all your diseases, who redeems your life
from the pit and crowns you with love and compassion,
who satisfies your desires with good things so that
your youth is renewed like the eagle's. . . .
He fulfills the desires of those who fear him.

(PSALM 103:1–5; 145:19A)

For just as through the disobedience
of the one man the many were made sinners,
so also through the obedience of the one man
the many will be made righteous.

ROMANS 5:19

CHAPTER 3

Men aren't jerks, they're fallen (like you)

My friend Tim met Jackie in the course of running errands one day. He was instantly smitten and pursued her with gusto. Tim couldn't wait to marry Jackie. The only reason he didn't propose within weeks of meeting her was that she wanted some time to get to know him. Though they still planned to marry, as time passed, things seemed to stall. Maybe Tim got used to the status quo; maybe they were getting too physical and so his desire was satisfied enough to remove a key incentive to marriage. For whatever reason, two years later, Tim finally sat down to have "the big talk." Only it wasn't a proposal. Even though by this time he'd already bought a one-carat engagement ring, something was preventing him from making the commitment and popping the question. Tim was stymied. "Maybe I'm just not ready to get married," he told Jackie. "Maybe I'm just too selfish. Besides, I like being single."

It's no wonder men have gained the collective reputation for being jerks.

The only problem with that conclusion is that all those jerks were created in the image of God. If, as sinners, men are jerks, so are we. And so are our parents, pastors, churches, and mentors. We all live in a fallen state. Romans 3:23 says, "For all have sinned and fall short of the glory of God." We all sin. It's just that at this historical point in our culture, men take the biggest rap for that sin. That, and the fact that most people no longer believe in the fall.

Despite all the evidence to the contrary, secularists insist sin is just a myth. They believe we are by nature good people and we have within us the ability to improve ourselves and to address any problems we see with our own strength, understanding, and whenever possible, a little social reengineering. Because they reject the reality of sin, their analysis of the problem and proposed solutions fall short. (Does anyone still think no-fault divorce, hooking up, and easy-access pornography are enlightened ideas?) The Bible gives us a different, true picture of the world. It's a story with three main acts: creation, fall, and redemption.

In our created, perfect state, God satisfied loneliness with marriage. And our desire for that companionship, not to mention sex, hasn't diminished all these generations later. What's different is our fallen attempts to try and satisfy those desires outside of marriage. True satisfaction lies in marrying well. But in order to have any reasonable chance of marrying well, we need to fully appreciate the effects of the fall. The initial chapters of this book looked at the created vision of marriage. This chapter is about the fall. It's not a fun topic, but without stopping briefly to understand it, we can't move on to what remains—redemption.

Our inborn drive should lead to earlier Christian marriage, but in our culture—where we've made sin an art—it rarely does.

Or at least not as often as it should. All generations have struggled under the curse of sin, but not every generation has struggled so greatly as ours in the area of marriage. Our grandparents and great-grandparents and those who preceded them had their share of hardships, but when it came to forming families, their box score was high. Something happened when it was our parents' turn. Starting with the baby boomers, the emphasis shifted from "marriage equals adulthood" to "marriage, nice if it happens" to "marriage, one of many lifestyle options." No longer do we assume we'll get married. And for many women, that life script is one they're not happy to abandon. On the whole, women still want to marry. And though most eventually will, they're doing so "later, less frequently, more hesitantly, and by and large, less successfully." So write Amy and Leon Kass in their anthology, *Wing to Wing, Oar to Oar*. When it comes to getting married, say the Kasses, "for the great majority the way to the altar is uncharted territory. It's every couple on its own bottom, without a compass, often without a goal. Those who reach the altar seem to have stumbled upon it by accident."[1]

The Kasses see such stumbling by their students at the University of Chicago. "We even detect among our students certain (albeit sometimes unarticulated) longings—for friendship, for wholeness, for a life that is serious and deep, and for associations that are trustworthy and lasting—longings that they do not realize could be largely satisfied by marrying well."[2]

There has never been a time when marriage was perfect. Ripples of the fall have affected every generation. But today's climate is unprecedented—what Maggie Gallagher and Linda Waite, in their book *The Case for Marriage*, call a "post marriage" culture. In another day, even nonbelievers married well. They knew intuitively that the benefits of marriage—for themselves and their children—were well worth the responsibilities. And that intuition shaped a culture that reinforced strong marriages.

But in our day, in the presence of so much cultural confusion, we've wandered from what God intended—the "ancient paths." When Israel did so, it was to their peril. God said,

"Because My people have forgotten Me,
they have burned incense to worthless idols.
And they have caused themselves to stumble
in their ways, from the ancient paths,
to walk in pathways and not on a highway,
to make their land desolate and a perpetual hissing;
everyone who passes by it will
be astonished and shake his head.

(*JEREMIAH* 18:15–16 NKJV)

It's like we've forgotten the simple, satisfying solution of marriage, and in a fog of amnesia, we reach for counterfeits: cohabitation, pornography, sex outside of marriage, homosexuality, friends with benefits. Is it any wonder Tim and Jackie are still single? The consequences of sin are far-reaching. In Psalm 78, the psalmist retells the history of Israel's rebellion against God, including God's responding curses. Not only do they endure disease and famine and military destruction, they also see a scourge on marriage; verse 63 says, "Fire consumed their young men, and their maidens had no wedding songs."

NOBODY'S BUSINESS?

Though we continue to crave relationships, our culture is skeptical of—and at points hostile toward—marriage. In the midst of the battles over marriage—what it is, who it includes, how it ends—a little-discussed change has taken place that is perhaps the most insidious of all. It's the one thing that has made all these other debates possible: the shift from marriage as objectively defined to marriage as subjective creation. For the marriage-minded, say Waite and Gallagher, this shift in definition harms us all. ". . . If we, as individuals, are to have the right to make this powerfully life-enhancing choice, we must first live in a society that respects, supports, enforces, and sustains the marriage vow. We must surrender the cherished myth, comforting to both the happily married and to the divorced, that our marriages are purely our own private creations, nobody's business but our own."[3]

We now know painfully well that in such a climate, divorce is normalized and, ultimately, commonplace. Though stable marriage—not the flimsy agreement they saw between their parents—remains a personal goal for young adults, they're "anxious about their ability to achieve it," say Waite and Gallagher, and less certain of marriage's unique ability to fulfill their relational needs. Consequently, "young Americans increasingly view marriage as just one of many equally acceptable relationship alternatives . . . alternatives [that] appear more reasonable and attractive."[4]

This cultural tolerance—even affirmation—of divorce, cohabitation, and sex outside of marriage creates a toxic environment where once the environment worked in favor of those who desired marriage. Waite and Gallagher state:

A simple but, we believe, true answer to the question of why marriage is in trouble is that Americans have invested less moral, spiritual, political, and legal energy into supporting the marriage vow. This reduced support for marriage expresses itself in a wide variety of relationships and institutions that touch the lives of married couples. Americans, for example, while no less eager for marriage, have become notably more enthusiastic about divorce and about other alternatives to marriage, from cohabitation to unwed childbearing.[5]

And I would add, "while no less eager for marriage," have forgotten how to help it happen.

FALLEN WOMEN

This is the culture we live in, but what we know more intimately is what happened in our own homes. Some of us experienced a shelter from the culture wars through parents who honored their vows and stayed married. Others, however—many others—were deeply wounded by parents who called it quits. More than 40 percent of all American adults between 18 and 40 are children of divorce, according to Jen Abbas in *Generation Ex*.[6] It's hard to shake that modeling. Even though the vast majority of young men and women in one study say having a good marriage and family life is "extremely important" to them, a much smaller number think it's likely they'll stay married to the same person for life.[7]

The Bible says marriage is good—even good for women—and research supports it. But that general truth seems like an abstraction for young women who saw that marriage wasn't good for their moms, moms who gave them a clear life script: "Don't let a man do to you what your dad did to me." And it wasn't just the moms who suffered. To young women left confused and abandoned by their fathers, their desire for men seems off-kilter and irrational.

How do women, in their fallen state, react to the damage? Instead of relating to men as their helpers, they view them as competitors; instead of viewing home as a noble responsibility, they shun it and look to the workplace as the only legitimate arena for their talents; instead of embracing their fertility, they debilitate it; instead of heeding wisdom's call, they hear only folly; and instead of becoming like a crown of glory to their husbands, they are a disgrace. Not a pretty sight. Maybe that's why it's so tempting to focus on the failures of men—it takes the focus off of us.

FALLEN MEN

Only when we've honestly grappled with our own fallenness can we look at men without despising them. They're reeling from the same divorce culture we are. And since divorce, regardless of who initiates it, almost always means dads recede from their children's lives, the boys often suffer more. Children of divorce typically live with mom, and though the single-parent home presents hardships all around, the sons are the ones who most often lose their same-sex role models. This is quite possibly the most tragic legacy of divorce: a generation of shiftless, underdeveloped, insecure men. And we wonder why men don't initiate.

I'm not giving them a pass. At some point, we all have to leave childish things behind—including forgiving for the things beyond our control—and accept adult responsibility. But I am convinced women need to understand the unique challenges men face in order to become the helpers God designed us to be. Most men since Adam have needed a woman's—a wife's—help. In order to help, we must back away from feminist hyperbole about the problem with men. Only then can we truly understand their sin. Like us, men in their fallen state are far from where God created them to be. Instead of sages, able to teach those they're responsible for, they trade the wisdom of God for the foolishness of the world; instead of learning skills and working hard to provide a good living, they squander their gifts and talents in selfish pursuits; instead of developing their physical strength to protect the weak, they use it to intimidate and dominate those most in need of their protection; and as image bearers of Christ, they scorn righteousness, living lives that lie about His true nature.

*F*ALLEN CHURCH

For these reasons and more, singles need help getting to marriage. But often the people they should be most able to count on for guidance—their church body—are themselves misguided in their understanding of what it means to help. "The body of Christ has so bought the lies of the world," says Dr. Del Tackett in *The Truth Project*, "that we have not only conformed to the world but we are suffering deeply from the consequences of believing those lies."[8]

Since 1960, we've witnessed radical shifts in the way we think about and treat men and women. Despite recent scientific "discoveries" about the differences between them, everything from kindergarten teachers to the military treats the sexes as the same. Distinctions between men and women have blurred. And the church is not immune.

Shortly before his death in 1984, Francis Schaeffer warned of churches trying to accommodate feminism:

Some evangelical leaders, in fact, have changed their views about inerrancy as a direct consequence of trying to come to terms with feminism. There is no other word for this than accommodation. It is a direct and deliberate bending of the Bible to conform to the world spirit of our age at the point where the modern spirit conflicts with what the Bible teaches.[9]

The effect on singles is especially damaging. The typical Single Adult Ministry does a good job covering topics like contentment, service, and discipleship—important things to study. Too often, though, they do it to the exclusion of what should be the defining life transition for most believers in their twenties and thirties. Less common are lessons about marriage, sex, and babies—topics that, to do them justice, would require different versions for men and women. When those groups do broach the subject of dating and marriage, it's tempting to camp out on the sovereignty of God with no mention of personal responsibility, saying, "Don't worry; if it's meant to be, He'll make it happen." What's worse is the implication: "If you do anything to encourage the process, you'll risk upsetting God's will for your life."

How did we get to this point? Some of the blame lies with the divorce explosion. Churches crafting messages to singles during the 1980s and 1990s were trying to address both categories of singles: divorced singles and never-marrieds. Never-married young adults have often been addressed with a script too similar to the one written for those who are "single again." And often that script includes negative comments about marriage, comments that create an extra level of anxiety and skepticism among never-marrieds.

Even a message designed specifically for never-marrieds doesn't work as "one size fits all." It's one thing to tell a woman to stop looking for a husband and just trust God to bring you one, but to tell a man to stop looking for a wife is a big part of why so many singles who'd like to be married aren't. To tell a man, "Stop looking for a wife and then she'll appear," is like telling him to stop studying, stop looking for a job, and stop house hunting in order to get a college degree, land a job, and buy a house. Sentiments like this may be well intentioned and even sound spiritual, but they're not biblical. Proverbs 18:22 says, "He who *finds a wife* finds what is good and receives favor from the Lord" (italics added). To find something—or in this case, someone—requires looking. Marriage is not a thing that's out looking for people to join. It's a state to be pursued. Ideally the one doing the pursuing is the man.

Why isn't there an outcry from within these groups, where the members remain single? Maybe it's because the messages they hear there, "Be the best single you can be and leave the rest to Him; You are complete in Jesus, etc," sound so compassionate. These sentiments undoubtedly flow from good intentions—the desire to make singles feel welcome and encouraged in their circumstances. And on their face, such comments and others like them sound like good advice. Especially when you consider how many men and women find themselves still single beyond their expectations through no apparent fault of their own. But in the end, they're not helpful. They don't do anything to move single women closer to their goal of marriage, a goal the majority of singles share. Eighty-six percent of American singles want to be married someday.[10] A majority of singles in churches are in a state of transition, and they still need the support of the local church in marrying well.

Such support is not only practical, but biblical. The role of the body is to encourage young men and women—all those who aren't specially gifted for celibate service—toward marriage. That includes more than mere words. It means practical advice for marrying well. In Titus 2:4–5, Paul instructs the older women to teach the younger women how to live godly lives. Specifically, "to love their husbands, to love their children, to be sensible, pure, workers at home, kind, being subject to their own husbands, so that the word of God will not be dishonored" (NASB). It only makes sense that if the young women are having trouble finding husbands in the first place, the older women have a vital role to play in helping them marry well.

WE ARE NOT WITHOUT HOPE

Redemption will not occur entirely in this world, but it can begin. The more we grasp our fallenness, the more we appreciate God's grace and redemptive purposes. And in a posture of gratitude, we open ourselves up to the possibilities of experiencing God's original design. Praise be to God our forgetfulness is not the end of the story. He does not abandon us. The invitation He issued to Israel in Jeremiah 6:16 still applies:

Thus says the Lord:
"Stand in the ways and see,
and ask for the old paths,
Where the good way *is,*
and walk in it;
then you will find rest
for your souls" (NKJV).

Let's journey together to rediscover the ancient paths.

God, the best maker of all marriages,
combine your hearts in one.

WILLIAM SHAKESPEARE, HENRY V

CHAPTER 4

God's still in the business of making good matches

A my was still recovering, but she was making progress. Only recently unattached again, she was at our house with some of her single friends talking about how she viewed her failed romance; the one she had thought would end, not with a breakup, but a proposal. "It was a roller-coaster ride," she said. "But now I can look back and see God's hand in each twist and turn. I believe He wanted me to go through all that to learn some things." Amy is a devout believer. But here she was, rationalizing a relationship that left her feeling jerked around and hurt, with no marriage to show for it. It's like she was casting God in her efforts to get married as some kind of cosmic puzzle maker—constructing a picture too mysterious and grand for her to really understand. Because she couldn't see the lid to the box with the picture of the completed puzzle, the best she could do was guess, after the fact, what He was up to. I believe God plays a much more benevolent role in our journey toward marriage.

"God takes a special and direct hand in one kind of marriage more than any other," says Barbara Mouser, author of *Five Aspects of Woman*. "This special wedding is the giving of a prudent woman."[1] She's talking about Proverbs 19:14. It says, "Houses and wealth are inherited from parents, but a prudent wife is from the Lord" (NASB). *The MacArthur Study Bible* interprets it this way: "A wise wife is a result of divine blessing." I just love the image of being given, by God, in marriage. He is not only aware of our desire for marriage; He is actively facilitating it for women who are wise. It's not something He did just for Adam and Eve. God is still in the business of making good matches.

The night before Steve and I got married, several of our friends charmed the guests at our rehearsal dinner with their personalized version of the song "Matchmaker" from *Fiddler on the Roof*. In honor of the couple everyone knew had been so instrumental in our romance, they sang "Match Morken, Match Morken, make me a match, find me a find, catch me a catch." We were the thirty-first couple the Morkens had helped toward the altar, and our friends weren't opposed to getting a little of that kind of help in their own lives.

Matchmakers go back a long way, longer than most of us realize. In Hebrew tradition, God is often described as the great *Shadchan*[2] or "marriage maker" who spends much of His time orchestrating marriages. It began when He made the first bride, Eve, and brought her to Adam to satisfy his longing. And it continues: while on earth, Jesus described marriage as "what God has joined together" (Matthew 19:6).

God as matchmaker. That has to be one of the most provocative ideas in the Bible for women who desire marriage. Provocative and inscrutable. One woman reads Proverbs 19:14 and says, "It's obvious God takes the lead on the work; there's not a whole lot I can do about getting married other than wait on Him." Another might say, "If it's prudent wives the Lord is giving to men, then I'd best get serious about being prudent."

All Him or all you. Both views are counterproductive. If it's all up to you, you're limited to your own wisdom, strength, and resources. If it's all up to God, you can lose sight of the possibility that what you do—or don't do—can undermine your chances of marrying well.

The effort to marry well is a shared one. Men have a significant role to play, as do your family and church community. While our fallenness has affected everyone's ability (including your own) to contribute their best to the symphony of making good marriages, we are not without hope. Someone in this score has remained faithful. "The plans of the Lord stand firm forever," wrote the psalmist, "the purposes of his heart through all generations" (Psalm 33:11). God hasn't changed. He's the same yesterday, today, and forever. It's our view that has changed, morphing right along with the culture around us. And when our understanding of God's role is flawed, our actions follow suit. Many women are missing out on God's best for their path to marriage precisely because they have a distorted sense of how their efforts, or lack thereof, intersect with His.

My friend Debbie, who decided to enlist the help of a matchmaker, ran into resistance from her well-meaning best friend. "Why don't you just chill out and take a year off and go to Venice? Who knows, you might meet someone there!" she said. Not one to trust in serendipity, Debbie quipped, "That is how you see God working? Me going to a foreign land where I know neither language nor culture, a Catholic bastion, and see if somewhere in the confusion, He can pair me up with a politically conservative, Reformed, professional type?"

"It's not that my friend was trying to be unhelpful," Debbie said, "but she had absorbed the notion that the harder we make it for God to pair us up, the greater the pairing will be. The further we place ourselves from marriage, that is when it will happen." Well, when you put it that way . . .

The woman who thinks it's all in her hands often faces heartache. It's not that she's *not* accomplished and used to getting whatever she sets her mind to, but that she *is*. Today's young women are arguably more educated, more resourceful, and more successful (financially, professionally) than any previous generation of women. That's why it's so frustrating when marriage doesn't happen on their timetable. Barbara Dafoe Whitehead talks about Christine, thirty, who has made it big in her career. She says, "By that age, she had expected to be married herself. Instead, she had already been in and out of relationships with seven different Mr. Not Readys. Her heart had been broken four times. It didn't make sense. Here she was, a woman who set goals for herself, met deadlines, accomplished all the things on her professional 'To Do' list, and yet she had missed a major 'To Do' in her life."[3] For women like Christine, unrealized relationship goals are a shock to their system.

So, too, the woman who thinks it's all up to God. I was that woman, convinced that the most I could do to help marriage along was beg God to bring me a husband, and soon. My frustration was no less than that of my friends who thought it was all up to them, but it differed in one key way. While they had only themselves to blame when it didn't happen, I had the added temptation of blaming God.

God is sovereign. He is all-powerful. He delights in giving good gifts to His children. All that and more is true. But none of it lets me off the hook for the things God has placed under my authority. I'm still responsible for a big part of the getting married equation. Much more than I realized. This was one of the most important things Mary Morken helped me to see. I had a role to play. God was working on my behalf; but for marriage to happen, I needed to cooperate with what He was doing. I had to take responsibility for the things that were under my control by God's design.

To suggest that *regardless of how you live*, God will bring the right man along when the time is right if marriage is His will, is at best naïve, and at worst presumptuous. The converse is also presumptive: that regardless of how you live, if marriage doesn't happen, it's because God didn't want it to. Every decision we make has consequences. And some of our decisions can keep us single. He is sovereign. But He gave us free will, and He will not contradict Himself to override our poor decisions. Barbara Mouser says, "God gave real authority to human creatures. There are five or six billion of us running loose in the world every day making decisions. . . . God does not undo every decision just because it is foolish or sinful. He lets most decisions stand. He does sometimes limit or keep things from happening through His providence. But He has given us real authority in this [earthly] domain, and He does not treat it lightly."[4]

We have the ability to undermine the good things God is trying to do on our behalf. I believe that's why so much of the book of Proverbs urges the reader to get wisdom. Solomon knew that a life lived the right way the first time was simply easier and more rewarding than one where every initial action and decision was foolish. Even if the fool eventually learned from her folly and reformed her ways, she still had to live with the consequences of her earlier wrong decisions. Under the new covenant, "Jesus forgives. But wisdom doesn't," says Mouser. The principles that order the natural realm aren't reversed simply because we've received forgiveness in the spiritual realm. Case in point: a woman who falls sexually will find forgiveness at the foot of the cross. Though she has a fresh start in the spiritual realm and is washed white as snow, the physical consequences of her sin—an STD, crisis pregnancy, or broken heart—remain.

Women who are appropriately waiting for guys to initiate still have plenty of things to *do*—as well as things to *stop doing*—to help marriage happen; all the while trusting God to play His part. And God's part is not small. If you're a believer, He's already done a great work on your behalf—work that transforms your life while helping you marry well.

He forgives your sins. First John 1:9 says, "If we confess our sins, he is faithful and just and will forgive us our sins and purify us from all unrighteousness." Ezekiel 36:26 says, "I will give you a new heart and put a new spirit in you." This gift pervades our life. It makes all things new. In the area of relationships, it makes it possible for you to unload the baggage of your past and move toward a healthy marriage with new hope and freedom.

He saves you from the world's way of doing things. God offers us—fallen men, women, parents, communities— a path of redemption through Christ. He begins to restore us in the roles He created us to play. Second Peter 1:3–4 tells us, "His divine power has given us everything we need for life and godliness through our knowledge of him who called us by his own glory and goodness. Through these he has given us his very great and precious promises, so that through them you may participate in the divine nature and escape the corruption in the world caused by evil desires."

He shows you how to live. If you have given God dominion of your life, He dwells in you and increases your wisdom. Colossians 1:27 says, "To them God has chosen to make known among the Gentiles the glorious riches of this mystery, which is Christ in you, the hope of glory."

His direction for your life becomes clear as you hide His Word in your heart and trust Him more than your own instincts. "Blessed are they who keep his statutes and seek him with all their heart. They do nothing wrong; they walk in his ways. . . . I rejoice in following your statutes as one rejoices in great riches" (Psalm 119:2–3, 14).

It's essential that you spend time reading and studying the Bible. Trouble is, that advice sounds a lot like "Eat less and get more exercise." In one ear and out the other. The difference is that fitness is good for life; God's Word *is* life. Proverbs 3:5–6 says, "Trust in the Lord with all your heart and lean not on your own understanding; in all your ways acknowledge him, and he will make your paths straight." By His Word, He'll light them (see Psalm 119:105).

Psalm 119, the really long one that used to throw me off (along with Leviticus and Ezekiel) when I was trying to read through the Bible in a year, is an elaborate tribute, heaping lavish praise on God's Word for its essence—it is the oxygen of godly living.

He meets your needs without harm. The menu of relationship options for women has expanded dramatically since the sexual revolution. Take your pick: "Urban Tribes," buddies, hookups, "friends with benefits," cohabitation, even lesbianism. All these arrangements and more promise pleasure, companionship, and sexual fulfillment. But none of them come close to the benefits and fulfillment found in a good marriage. And what's worse, they do more harm than good. It's freeing to realize that God's way is best after all, even for those who don't acknowledge Him. He provided marriage, along with the parameters that distinguish it from other relationships, as a common grace gift to all who enter it. Over the years, billions of people have embraced marriage and reaped the resulting benefits.

He helps you resist temptation. Still, many forgo marriage and choose instead one of the many relationship aberrations. Even with mounting evidence of their negative consequences, they seem appealing. Why? Because they promise the benefits of marriage without the risks and responsibilities. It goes back to our fallen nature; our desire for forbidden fruit. The Enemy is working overtime to sever the connection between the joys of marriage and the parameters God put around it, tempting us with pseudo-relationships and especially the short-term pleasures of premarital sex. First Peter 5:8 says, "Be self-controlled and alert. Your enemy the devil prowls around like a roaring lion looking for someone to devour." One of the best ways God helps us toward marriage is by giving us the ability to resist the temptations that undermine it (Hebrews 2:18; and 1 Corinthians 10:13).

God's Word gives you the road map to relational fulfillment. But having a map is pointless if you keep it folded up in your glove box. You have to get it out, open it up, study it, follow it. You have to act on the reality that regardless of your circumstances, your doubts and fears, and what the culture says, God's way—covenantal marriage—is trustworthy.

Never-married women are a lot like Peter walking on the water. Having confirmed that it was Jesus, and not a ghost, coming toward them, Peter had the confidence to get out of the boat and join Jesus in a miraculous stroll. "But when [Peter] saw the wind," the Scripture says, "he was afraid and, beginning to sink, cried out, 'Lord, save me!' Immediately Jesus reached out his hand and caught him. 'You of little faith,' he said, 'why did you doubt?'" (Matthew 14:3–31). It wasn't that the wind suddenly appeared, throwing Peter off. The storm had already been raging. It was that he suddenly shifted his focus from Jesus to the weather. He lost sight of what was most important—God's presence in the midst of the storm. Our culture is like that storm. To survive it, we have to keep our gaze on Christ regardless of what's going on around us.

In *The Truth Project*, Del Tackett asks what he calls "a haunting question": Do you really believe that what you believe is really real? While you may have known about God for most of your life, are you living like you believe He is who He says He is?

Have you applied the reality of His truth, love, power, wisdom, forgiveness, and redemption to every area of your life, including your relationships with men?

DOES GOD NEED US?

With God doing so much on our behalf, why do anything? He certainly doesn't lack ability, power, or even incentive (see Malachi 2:15). It's tempting to think any action on our part will risk getting in His way. Besides, men are the ones who are supposed to initiate. They're the ones who are supposed to be out *finding* wives (Proverbs 18:22). Doesn't activity on our part as women show a lack of faith?

There's a biblical precedent for waiting on the Lord. Exodus 14:14 says, "The Lord will fight for you; you need only to be still." Psalm 37:7 says, "Be still before the Lord and wait patiently for him." And the classic comfort to singles, Jeremiah 29:11 says, " 'For I know the plans that I have for you,' declares the Lord, 'plans for welfare and not for calamity to give you a future and a hope' " (NASB).

My favorite was Jeremiah 29:11. I wrote it on a Post-it note and stuck it to my mirror. A lot of my single friends did too. We drew great comfort from the idea that God had marriage in mind for us even when it seemed like a remote possibility. Ironically, it wasn't until after I was married that Steve and I spent some time studying that verse in its context. Beginning with verse 4, Jeremiah said, "This is what the Lord Almighty, the God of Israel, says to all those I carried into exile from Jerusalem to Babylon: 'Build houses and settle down; plant gardens and eat what they produce. Marry and have sons and daughters; find wives for your sons and give your daughters in marriage, so that they too may have sons and daughters. Increase in number there; do not decrease' " (vv. 4–6).

God's still in the business of making good matches   75

God had a good plan for the exiles in Babylon, but it required their active participation—getting married, having babies, building houses, planting gardens. In fact, it was the exiles' faithfulness in getting married and having children that maintained the lineage of the Messiah and revealed the best part of the plan God had for them. As encouraging as verse 11 was, it would have been even more so if I'd read what preceded it to realize the hope and future it promised was a direct result of them taking the active step of marrying and having children!

And that verse from Exodus 14? Right after Moses tells the people to be still, God Himself asks, "Why are you crying out to me? Tell the Israelites to move on." I don't remember hearing many sermons on the activity God required in verse 15.

As for Psalm 37, starting with verse 1, David wrote,

Do not fret because of evil men or be envious
of those who do wrong; for like the grass they will
soon wither, like green plants they will soon die away.
Trust in the Lord and do good; dwell in the land
and enjoy safe pasture. Delight yourself in the Lord
and he will give you the desires of your heart. Commit
your way to the Lord; trust in him and he will do this:
he will make your righteousness shine like the dawn,
the justice of your cause like the noonday sun. Be still
before the Lord and wait patiently for him; do not
fret when men succeed in their ways, when they
carry out their wicked schemes (vv. 1–7).

Preceding God's admonition to "be still" is His encouragement to "*trust,* " "*do* good," "*dwell* in the land," "*delight,*" "*commit* your way to the Lord." A whole list of verbs. God calls us to be still when we are tempted to follow the shortcuts of the wicked, but active when it comes to trusting and obeying the ways He has set out before us; believing that His ways are best and result in His blessings.

The tension in these passages between rest and activity suggests we have a role to play in God's work, even at points where we're told to be still. While God plays a large part in our marrying well, He doesn't intend for us to leave everything in His hands. Proverbs 21:31 says, "The horse is made ready for the day of battle, but victory rests with the Lord." A soldier with an untrained, malnourished horse won't be much good to his regiment. The victory, though attributable to God, would be unlikely if all the soldiers neglected their steeds. The point of that verse is not "no matter what the soldiers do or don't do, victory is inevitable." The point is that the soldiers do all they can to prepare, recognizing the limits of their responsibility and credit. The victory, if it happens, is the Lord's.

So it is with us. Women must do all they can to prepare. Then we can trust God for the rest, knowing we've been faithful to do our part. When I met Steve, the steed that was my life needed some getting ready. There were areas that I'd neglected (my eating habits, fitness, and checkbook—I had to stop, for example, assuming I'd marry a doctor and he'd make all my irresponsible spending disappear), and some that I'd conformed to the world's standards (my clothes, makeup, and attitude toward men). God used my desire for marriage to shape my character, soften my approach, reform my spending, and shrink my waistline. These weren't easy changes to make, but they were good ones; consistent with my role as steward. They laid the groundwork for a healthy perspective that would serve my future husband and family well.

So which is it, God working or us working? Often, it's God working through us. In his book *God at Work*, Gene Edward

Veith Jr. describes the doctrine of vocation. It is, as Martin Luther described it, a picture of God working through means. The following extended passage shows eloquently how our work intersects with God's:

When we pray the Lord's Prayer, observed Luther, we ask God to give us this day our daily bread. And He does give us our daily bread. He does it by means of the farmer who planted and harvested the grain, the baker who made the flour into bread, the person who prepared our meal. . . .

Before you ate, you probably gave thanks to God for your food, as is fitting. He is caring for your physical needs, as with every other kind of need you have, preserving your life through His gifts. . . . And He does so by using other human beings. *It is still God who is responsible for giving us our daily bread* [emphasis added]. Though He could give it to us directly, by a miraculous provision, as He once did for the children of Israel when He fed them daily with manna, God has chosen to work through human beings, who, in their different capacities and according to their different talents, serve each other. This is the doctrine of vocation.

To use another of Luther's examples, God could have decided to populate the earth by creating each new person from the dust, as He did Adam. Instead, He chose to create new life through the *vocation* of husbands and wives, fathers and mothers. . . .

When we or a loved one gets sick, we pray for healing. Certainly God can and sometimes does grant healing through a miracle. But normally He grants healing through the vocations of doctors, nurses, pharmacists, lab technicians, and the like. It is still God who heals us, but He works through the means of skilled, talented, divinely equipped human beings. When God blesses us, He almost always does it through other people.[5]

God is sovereign. And God works through means. It's as if God does a heavenly handoff to provide for our needs. This is a great reminder that God is not only at work when He's performing supernatural miracles, but that He's also at work when we are living out the natural processes He established. We get our bread from the hand of God through the hands of all the people who had a role in making it possible.

Just as with bread, I believe God provides husbands and wives for those who desire to marry. Ultimately, it's God who brings us a mate. But not the way He dropped manna from heaven. This is a book about means—about how God can provide marriage through the work of our lives and those around us—not in a frenzy of desperate activity, but in a symphony of faithfulness among a community of believers pursuing the lives God has called us to live.

It's the Network.

BESPECTACLED VERIZON SUPPORT GUY

CHAPTER 5

You need a network

W hat are your intentions for my daughter?"
That's what my dad asked Steve during his first
visit to my hometown. Steve was a captive audience;
sitting nervously in my dad's dental chair, my dad
hovering over Steve's open mouth with a whirring drill. Steve
was sweating. But then my dad smiled. Always one for a good
joke, his chuckle let Steve off the hook.

How does the idea of your dad interviewing your boyfriend
make you feel? What's your emotional reaction to the picture
of your dad asking a guy you like about his intentions for
you—your future together—before the first date even starts?
Repulsion? Fear that no guy in his right mind would sit still
for such an interrogation? Anxiety that you'd never have a date
again? Thankful for a dad who cares enough to get involved?
Hope for that level of concern and involvement by a dad with
your best interests at heart?

In another day, regardless of how you felt about it, your dad would have asked that question in all seriousness. And he wouldn't have moved, nor let your planned date begin, until the young man came up with a satisfying answer. Parents used to be very active in their daughters' preparation for marriage, their opportunities for worthy suitors, their protection from rascals. The parents' blessing was essential to launching a new relationship; their ongoing support a vital part of their daughter's new marriage.

That's rarely the case anymore. Parents have watched their role diminish to little more than paying for the wedding when it does finally happen. What was once a responsibility squarely on their shoulders has been taken away, abandoned, and recast. Taken away by a culture that prizes romance above all else. Abandoned by parents in the face of their own dwindling confidence in their ability to shepherd the dating process. And recast as belonging exclusively in the hands of the women—their daughters—they once worked so hard to protect.

Aside from "mild teasing pressure from parents who want grandchildren,"[1] anymore it's an exception to find a father or mother who feels responsible for helping their daughters (and sons) marry well. Even among Christians, there's a sense that parents should be hands off, including those areas where their daughters would appreciate their involvement. Parents with good intentions—I'd include my dad in that category—still want to do what they can to help their daughters, but they no longer have a script, cultural or personal, to follow. In most cases they're left with nothing more than the modeling—however flawed—of their parents' or their own dating histories.

Of late there's been a quirky resurgence of parental involvement. But these so-called "helicopter parents" are primarily concerned about education and career decisions. Ironically, a dad who's bold enough to call a college registrar to demand entrance for his obviously "gifted" daughter is loathe to call a man who could change the course of the rest of her life to ask what his intentions are.

What has parental disengagement gotten us? Women in assorted states of singleness stretching out beyond their expectations; skyrocketing rates of premarital sex and babies born out of wedlock,[2] no longer two identified STDs but twenty-five,[3] rampant cohabitation, and more. It's hard to prove causation, but I think the case can be made. It's like what happened when the Supreme Court took prayer out of the public schools. With prayer, "the top seven disciplinary problems were: talking in class, chewing gum, making noises, running in the halls, cutting in line, improper clothing, and not disposing of garbage. Today, recent surveys are frightening. The top seven disciplinary problems are: rape, robbery, assault, burglary, arson, bombing, murder."[4]

While making this very point during his Renewing American Civilization course, historian and political leader Newt Gingrich was challenged by one of his students. The young man wanted to know how taking a vanilla, nonsectarian prayer away from the start of the school day could really cause all that havoc. Could such a seemingly minor change have such a huge effect on students' behavior? Gingrich explained that when you remove the presence of an authority greater than the teacher, classroom management and discipline is as weak or strong as each individual teacher. No longer were students reminded of that overarching authority. Teachers were left to their own abilities, without a backup.

So it is for single women. They've been abandoned, left to fend for themselves when it comes to getting married. For better or worse, they're all they have. No longer do young men dating young women recognize any authority or protection in the equation. It's just the guy and his date. No questions asked. No one waiting up for her to make curfew. "For the first time in human history," writes Leon Kass, "mature women by the tens of thousands live the entire decade of their twenties—their most fertile years—neither in the homes of their fathers nor in the homes of their husbands; unprotected, lonely, and out of sync with their inborn nature. Some women positively welcome this state of affairs, but most do not; resenting the personal price they pay for their worldly independence, they nevertheless try to put a good face on things and take refuge in work or feminist ideology."[5]

While some parents are showing renewed interest in their daughters' struggles to marry well, most women still face the challenge of going it alone. If you're one of the few with a dad who is trying to follow a biblical model, you're blessed. Thank him and allow him to live out the responsibility God has called him to. If you don't have that support, you can ask for it. If your dad says he's up for helping, but isn't sure what to do, suggest a plan. Together you could read *Boy Meets Girl* by Joshua Harris and *Her Hand in Marriage* by Douglas Wilson. Encourage him to spend time with your suitor(s) one-on-one. Your dad may have much to offer young men in the form of his friendship and counsel. Best of all, the man you end up marrying will already have a solid foundation with your dad; something that will bless your marriage later on.

After years of following the world's way, my friend Christine decided to ask her dad to get involved. Here's how it played out in her story:

> Just months after I started rethinking how I went about dating, I met Richard. Here was this guy who from the looks of things had everything I wanted in a mate—everything I had ever dreamed of. There was chemistry from the beginning, and I was tempted to carry on as I always had. Then I remembered the

get married

promises I had made to God, and I also remembered the hurts of the past. Sitting in the car after a very romantic date when the rain was beating down outside and sparks were going off inside, I took the very bold step of laying everything on the line. It was a huge risk. I was a twenty-six-year-old woman telling a thirty-year-old man I barely knew that I didn't believe in dating, but in courtship. I told him that not only did I think it wasn't good to kiss, but that (horror above horrors) I wanted to invite our parents to take part in our relationship. It was a paralyzing two minutes for me that I'll never forget. When he finally responded with a smile and an astonished, "Wow, well, I think we could try something like that," I couldn't believe it.

It was mostly my parents who participated initially. I sent them a copy of the book that had changed my perspective about dating so they could read and see for themselves the kind of role I was envisioning for them. They were typical in that they prayed for me and talked to me but were hesitant to offer too much guidance. The burden really was on me to ask them to hold us accountable and to open the door to full communication about our relationship. Both of them were pleased to participate. My mom and I have a close relationship and always talked about "future husbands," but my dad didn't discuss such things with me very much. I think the simple fact that I asked him to take part made him realize just how serious I was about this guy and was therefore willing to rise to the occasion.

Richard still jokes about the day he sat in a chair across from my parents "without food or water" and was interrogated for hours on end. They asked question upon question about his faith and family background, vision for the future, hopes, and ambitions. It was an unusual and unlikely experience for us all, but it seemed that through the discomfort we established a level of decorum and respect that had not been present in past relationships.

Richard's parents are British and not as comfortable being open about personal affairs with people they don't know well, so the dynamics with them were a little different. I think just telling them about how we planned to approach our relationship made them realize that we were both committed to honoring a high code of conduct. It naturally made them think it was something to be taken seriously. They became deliberate about getting to know me and sharing who they were. We weren't attempting to bond as in-laws, just trying to understand more about who the other was and enjoy that for what it was.

It was really hard for both of us to take this new approach, but it turned out to be the best thing we could have done. Richard surprised me by actually leading the way in this new model, which demonstrated to me a depth of character that I hadn't known in a man before. His willingness to "hold back" before we were married established a level of trust between us that I still look back to for reassurance when challenges come our way. Had I not chosen the difficult task of applying "delayed gratification," who knows where I'd be today!

Proverbs says, "There is wisdom in the counsel of many," and it's the wise woman who seeks the counsel of her parents, even when it's a little uncomfortable and embarrassing.

If getting one or both of your parents involved is not an option—whether for reasons of death, divorce, geographic distance, different faith convictions, or simply lack of interest—you're not without hope

ENTORS

Paul provided a remedy in the advice he gave in Titus 2. Speaking about the range of ages in any church body, he encouraged the older believers to counsel the younger ones. Getting wisdom from someone who's further down the road is invaluable. Even if their journey's been a bumpy one—maybe even more so—they're better able to provide scouting than your peers.

It's far trendier, and less awkward, to seek the advice and help of your friends. But when it comes to finding a husband, older women, and couples, have a lot more help to offer. Not only do they have wisdom, and possibly even names of eligible bachelors, they also have a wealth of life experience to share about everything from education and career choices, church involvement, cultural discernment, and political activity to candid advice about health and beauty. It's like having a mom who's dispassionate (not a bad thing when you're talking about your eating habits, clothing choices, and hairstyle).

My friend Sharon's mentor challenged her in a way that she says, "changed my life." Sharon, a cute, petite blonde with piercing blue eyes, admitted that though she was a few years past college, she still dressed like a student. "I preferred jeans and baggy sweatshirts or university tees," Sharon said. Her mentor called her to a higher standard. "She challenged me in the most loving yet bold way I have ever been challenged. She challenged the way I dressed and how I cared for myself. She said I should dress like a woman. She encouraged me to take care of my body by eating better and exercising. And she challenged me to read the Bible every day of my life. Some may have seen it as harsh, but I was and am so thankful for her investment in my life. Through her life I saw in a new way how what you wear affects how people perceive and react to you. And taking her advice,

I felt better about myself. I realized through this process that the kind of fish you catch depends on the kind of bait you put on the hook. I want to be the kind of woman who is filled with the Word of God, and I want my future husband to be the same way."

And it's not just what mentors know, but whom. If you only spend time with people in the same season of life you're in, the competition for available men will likely be fierce. But if your friends span the generations, it's probable they will know or be related to eligible men. And if these friends are believers in marriage—and they know you have marriage as a goal— they can be helpful allies. You never know where a mentor's insights in the form of advice, open doors, and introductions may lead.

Research by the National Marriage Project confirms this. Their annual report for 2004 says,

The most likely way to find a future marriage partner is through an introduction by family, friends, or acquaintances. Despite the romantic notion that people meet and fall in love through chance or fate, the evidence suggests that social networks [the old-fashioned kind] are important in bringing together individuals of similar interests and backgrounds, especially when it comes to selecting a marriage partner. According to a large-scale national survey of sexuality, almost 60 percent of married people were introduced by family, friends, co-workers or other acquaintances.[6]

Do the people in your life know you desire marriage? Do they know the qualities you're seeking in a husband? They might be willing accomplices in the search—and even helpful ones at that. Start to pray for and seek out mentors. Look for older married couples you can spend time with. Ask them to pray with and for you about your desire for marriage. And if they worry that they don't know any eligible bachelors right now, reassure them that it doesn't mean they won't meet one in the future.

This kind of "help" carries certain risks, and you wouldn't want to be introduced to just any available male. That's why it's important to pray about whom you approach for mentoring. One of the keys to a successful mentoring relationship is finding a person, or people, who have strengths in the area you are trying to improve. In the case of mentoring toward marriage, that means approaching a woman whose own godly life gives her the credibility to speak into yours. Some women still bear the scars of the feminist revolution. Some are still bitter over their own failed marriages. One good test is how a woman reacts to Genesis 2 and Ephesians 5. Because you're seeking help for marriage, what a potential mentor believes about marriage—and how she lives it out in her own life—matters.

When I worked on Capitol Hill, I met a woman whose career I greatly admired. She was a bold success in her job and yet managed to remain feminine. I wanted to learn from her and so I asked her to mentor me in the area of my job. She was not, however, the woman who could help me in my desire for a husband—she was a longtime single. That advice came from another woman, someone whose life affirmed Christian marriage. And for help learning how to be a godly mom, I've looked to yet another woman. Each of these three women has distinct skills and areas of maturity that I've wanted to emulate at different seasons of my life.

Once you've identified someone you look up to who would be a good fit for this role, it's important to ask her if she's willing to mentor you. Make it official, says mentoring expert Bobb Biehl, author of *Mentoring*. Doing so creates opportunities for serious discussion and deep questions that might feel inappropriate in casual conversations. He suggests approaching a potential mentor and saying something like, "I would like you to consider being one of my life mentors." "In seeking a mentor," he says, "don't hesitate—initiate."[7]

Beyond that, I think regular and casual is the way to go. Mentoring is different from discipleship, which is highly structured and driven by the teacher. Think of this as a friendship with someone you look up to and respect. The less structured the relationship, the less intimidated both of you will be about spending time together and allowing issues to come up naturally. That doesn't mean you shouldn't have a regular time set to meet each week or biweekly or monthly (whatever works with your schedules), but when you do meet, you're not working through a formal curriculum. Meet for coffee, take walks, discuss books you're reading, talk about what God is showing you in Scripture, tell her what's currently weighing on your heart, and let her encourage you, pray with you, and when necessary, challenge you.

When you do start dating, make a point to spend time as a couple with your mentor(s). Hopefully the man you are dating will have a mentor, or be open to having one too. Getting input from a seasoned married couple will help keep your dating relationship on the right track. If the man isn't a good fit, figuring that out early will spare you a lot of heartache and wasted time. If what you're after is a strong, healthy marriage relationship, strong healthy relationships within your Christian community are the best way to get there.

THE CHURCH

Are you in a church body where you can find such a mentor couple?

Singles in their twenties and thirties are much less likely to be active members of a church body than other population segments,[8] but it's in these formative and transitional years that you most need to be in a fellowship of believers—especially if you hope to marry well.

There's a lot I could say about churches and marriage, but I'll just hit a couple of key points.

First, the marriage climate of a church starts in the pulpit. Strong, biblical teaching that honors marriage, purity, relational integrity, and distinct biblical gender roles can help nurture a climate conducive to fruitful mentoring, good matches, and healthy marriages.

Of course, the opposite is also true. When pastors shy away from addressing marriage, sexual purity, and courtship—or if the only time they address singles is in the context of "it's better not to marry" or "don't make marriage an idol"—that also affects the church climate. In such settings, it's more likely women will be left on their own to navigate a dating scene that's not very distinct from the culture. Or worse, it can lead to the guys hiding behind spiritual fig leaves in an attempt to justify self-centered pseudo-relationships.

Second, you might need to ask the church for relational help if it isn't already providing it. Church consumer research might be telling your pastor that singles don't want to hear about marriage—that they just want to hear about being fulfilled in their singleness and growing in their faith. As a result, your church may have scaled back on programming they once offered for those who were marriage-minded. Churches are more likely to consider such a service if they get enough feedback that a need exists. Letting your pastor know you need vision and preparation for marriage, especially if a few of your single friends join you in the conversation, will create a good opportunity to see how your church views their role in helping singles marry well.

Finally, it's valuable to include a pastor or a lay leader in your "relationship network" once you meet someone and start dating toward marriage. A spiritual leader can add an extra dimension to the advice, modeling, and accountability you receive from your parents and mentors.

"The pastor of the church I attended in Washington, D.C., was a godsend to me when the single season of my life was coming to a close," said Christine. "Richard and I had been dating for a few months, and he was everything I had been looking for in a mate. But I was upset to discover the sky-high feelings of being 'in love' beginning to wane. I started wondering if I had been wrong to think Richard was 'the one' for me. My pastor listened patiently to my tales of woe and then said something I'll never forget: 'Relationships ebb and flow; what's important is that this guy carries the qualities and characteristics of the godly man you've been waiting for.' That sentence gave me extra confidence to move forward despite my feelings, or lessening thereof, and was really reassuring for me."

It's also important to make an early connection with a pastor in the church where you plan to marry. Increasingly, couples are getting premarital counseling—of course, it's often because churches are requiring it before performing ceremonies in their facilities. Friends of mine who counsel couples tell me, however, that it's better if couples go through premarital counseling or education before they actually get engaged. Once they set a date, it's too easy to have all of their attention focused on the wedding details, making it tempting to minimize any problems that emerge, instead of giving them the attention they need. All the more so if the problems are serious.

In discussing the church body, Paul wrote, "And if one member suffers, all the members suffer with it; if one member is honored, all the members rejoice with it" (1 Corinthians 12:26 NASB). The stories I hear leave me to think there are a lot of suffering single church members. It's my prayer that as single women are more intentional about their place in the body and more forthright about their need for help to prepare for marriage, that local churches will find ways to honor those needs in a way that all the members can rejoice.

"It's the network," says one Verizon Wireless campaign, picturing a man with his cell phone being followed around by a massive crew of telecom support staff. The implication: With Verizon you're never on your own. You have a team behind you guaranteeing the success of every call you make. Getting married in our culture requires that kind of support. Backed by a team of parents, mentors, pastors, and friends, the women who marry well would likely say, "It's the network."

Wake up, O sleeper, rise from the dead,
and Christ will shine on you.

EPHESIANS 5:14

CHAPTER 6

Waking a great sleeper

I think I may have raised my daughter to be lonely."
That's what a friend of mine said during our conversation
about the seeming famine of eligible Christian men. I
can't say that I blame her. Her daughter is lovely, smart,
and talented—like a lot of women I know. And they're all having
trouble finding guys of equal caliber.

Maybe it has something to do with our perception of quality
single men—specifically, the lack of them. Popular singles writers
have cited a Barna finding about Christian women outnumbering
Christian men. And in this case, it's no small gap. The number
I've heard referenced and seen in print is that there are between
eleven and thirteen million *more* single Christian women than
there are single Christian men. Can this be true?

What does Barna himself say about Christian men and
women? According to his website, as of the year 2000: "The
survey data show that nearly half of the nation's women have
beliefs [that] classify them as born again (46 percent), compared

to just about one-third of men (36 percent). In other words, there are between 11 million and 13 million more born again women than there are born again men in the country."[1]

The first thing I noticed is that Barna is talking about *all* Christian men and women—not just singles. The second is that the stat is outdated. It was published in 2000, and Barna's 2006 numbers show the gap is narrowing. Even though the percentage of born-again women has swelled to 49 percent, the percentage of men has gone up too: 41 percent of men now describe themselves as born again. That change alone shrinks the deficit between Christian men and women to something like ten million.

So who are those ten million women? Are they the young never-marrieds who feel outnumbered at church? The ones citing the depressing stats? When you look closely at the numbers, you find that much of the gap between the number of Christian men and women is simply due to healthy women outliving their husbands. Christian widows outnumber Christian widowers four to one. Another category in which Christian women outnumber Christian men is the divorced—but even that gap is much more modest.

So what about Christians who have never married? The surprising reality is that there are more men than women—a lot more. The 2006 Statistical Abstract of the United States identified 29,561,000 never-married men compared to 23,655,000 never-married women—*that's almost six million more never-married men than women.*[2] The Barna Group estimates that 48 percent of never-married men are believers and 52 percent of never-married women are. Applying those estimates to the Census numbers,[3] you end up with nearly two million more never-married Christian men than never-married Christian women. Is that true of only some age categories? Does the surplus of men only exist on college campuses, among twentysomethings, but nowhere else? Surprisingly, the only age segment where never-married women outnumber never-married men is among those seventy-five and older—which is also tied to greater life expectancy for women.

Yet every time I've heard the "more women than men" stat cited it's in the context of never-married women bemoaning their chances of finding a mate. If we're trying to get a sense of a never-married Christian woman's probability of getting married to a Christian man, we've got to honestly (and I'd say with a sigh of relief) admit women have the advantage.

WHERE THE MEN ARE

At least now we can move on from the fallacy that there simply aren't enough men to go around. Barna's study did find that more single women than single men are in church. So we're left wondering how to find them. If all these Christian men aren't in church on Sunday morning, where are they?

The short answer is Bozeman, Montana. You might also consider Cullman, Alabama, or Ames, Iowa. According to the Census Bureau, they're among the cities with the biggest gap between single men and women. But who's ready to pack up and move to Bozeman? Thankfully, in almost every region of the country there are more never-married men than women. The overall national ratio of men to women (unmarried, ages fifteen to forty-four years) is 108.7 men to 100 women. Only two states—Mississippi and Louisiana—have more unmarried women than men. And even in those two states, the numbers are close (ninety-eight men for every one hundred women). The District of Columbia ranks pretty low at 93.4 men for every 100 women, but even that area favors men when you add in the metro area around the city (105.7 men to 100 women).[4]

While you may increase your odds of marrying by casting around for men in some male-dominated regions of the country, the fact remains that there are plenty of men to go around *right where you are*.

I feel like celebrating. There are plenty of males to go around.

But are they actually interested in marriage? Surprisingly, more so than women. A 2006 Pew Internet study found single men were more likely than single women to be in a committed relationship (30 percent to 23 percent). Though 42 percent of single men said they weren't in a committed relationship and weren't looking for a partner, 65 percent of single women said the same thing. Fully 23 percent of single men said they were looking for a partner while only nine percent of women did.[9]

The Pew study didn't ask about faith, but a similar study by the Centers for Disease Control did. They found that in general, more men than women agreed with the statement, "It is better to get married than to go through life being single." This was also true by a large margin between men and women who said religion is very important as well as those categorized as Fundamentalist Protestant.[6]

So you're thinking, *If there are more than enough men right where I am who actually want to get married, why am I still single?*

Because you're out for more than just a warm male body (or should be). Beyond numbers is character. There may be a lot more single Christian guys than we realized, but that doesn't change the fact that a lot of them haven't exactly embraced their calling to be strong leaders, providers, or protectors. Yes, there are lots of guys. But where are the *men?*

In a word, sleeping. Most of the men in our culture haven't had any high expectations to meet. By and large they've endured an education system that treats them like girls and medicates them when they act like boys. Few have strong role models. And so they're passive. Thankfully there are things you can do to encourage single male believers in their role as initiator. One of the greatest motivators is your belief. What men need is to have someone who believes in them more than they believe in themselves. They need women who see in them, and encourage, what God designed men to be before the fall. Your respect is what leads to his pursuit.

As much as women clamor for role-less relationships—interchangeable job descriptions, so to speak—what they really want, at least most women, most of the time, is a *man*. And a man leads. A man is strong and willing to sacrifice and take on responsibility and risk. And therein lies the rub. Risk is well, risky. It's hard. It's painful. And it often ends in failure. But that's what a man is supposed to do. He's supposed to risk. For you, and down the road, for you and your children.

DISCERN HIS CHARATER

For this reason, it's essential that you test his character. If it's strong, or potentially so, you know you're making a worthy investment of time and affection in your relationship with him. If it's not, you can avoid wasting precious time on a relationship that likely won't, and shouldn't, lead to marriage.

Proverbs 20:5 says, "The purposes of a man's heart are deep waters." How can you plumb those depths; how can you really know if he's capable of lifelong commitment—especially in just a few months—in a culture where men are primarily judged for their ability to show women a good time? Aside from essential input from parents, mentors, and your church body, how can you know for yourself if you're dating the genuine article: a man capable of marriage and worthy of your respect? Start with Scripture.

Ephesians 5:1–7 says,

Be imitators of God, therefore, as dearly loved children
and live a life of love, just as Christ loved us and gave himself
up for us as a fragrant offering and sacrifice to God. But among
you there must not be even a hint of sexual immorality, or of
any kind of impurity, or of greed, because these are improper
for God's holy people. Nor should there be obscenity, foolish

talk or coarse joking, which are out of place, but rather thanksgiving. For of this you can be sure: No immoral, impure or greedy person—such a man is an idolater—has any inheritance in the kingdom of Christ and of God. Let no one deceive you with empty words, for because of such things God's wrath comes on those who are disobedient. Therefore do not be partners with them.

Once you've measured his current behavior against this standard (assuming you've already done the same with your own behavior), consider the details that follow about what his role will be as a husband (and yours as his wife):

Wives, submit to your husbands as to the Lord.
For the husband is the head of the wife as Christ is
the head of the church, his body, of which he is the Savior.
Now as the church submits to Christ, so also wives
should submit to their husbands in everything.

Husbands, love your wives, just as Christ loved the church and gave himself up for her to make her holy, cleansing her by the washing with water through the word, and to present her to himself as a radiant church, without stain or wrinkle or any other blemish, but holy and blameless. In this same way, husbands ought to love their wives as their own bodies. He who loves his wife loves himself. After all, no one ever hated his own body, but he feeds and cares for it, just as Christ does the church—for we are members of his body. "For this reason a man will leave his father and mother and be united to his wife, and the two will become one flesh." This is a profound

get married

mystery—but I am talking about Christ and the church. However, each one of you also must love his wife as he loves himself, and the wife must respect her husband.

(EPHESIANS 5:22–33)

That last bit about respect causes a lot of grumbling among women with feminist leanings. But we ignore it to our own harm. Even apart from the fact that God's Word requires it, sociological research affirms it. Men empirically need respect the way women need love. Emerson Eggerichs writes about the findings in his book *Love and Respect*. Studies have shown that men who feel the genuine respect of their wives are better husbands, and their wives are happier women. Marriages marked by the unconditional giving of love and respect thrive. That's why it's so important that you marry a man you can respect.

It's not just the "husband and wife" passages that reveal a man's character. The whole Word does. Proverbs 20:27 says, "The lamp of the Lord searches the spirit of a man; it searches out his inmost being."

Our first Christmas together, Steve gave me a *One Year Bible*. I know I should have been happier with it than I was. But I couldn't help thinking, *Not very romantic*. Glad I didn't say that out loud. Steve's interaction with and response to God's Word was the best way for me to know what was in his heart. I knew he had his own copy and it really was a wise gift. Now we'd both be reading the same portions of Scripture at the start of each day. That created lots of opportunities to talk about what we were reading and what we believed about it. In retrospect, I can't imagine a better gift for a newly dating couple trying to discern if they are in what Barbara Mouser calls "the same spiritual weight class" and if they should move toward marriage.

Beyond Scripture, there are surprisingly many opportunities to test a man's character in the course of conversation. In my experience, one of the best ways to do that is to head to the movies. Why movies? Because they create an opportunity to discuss things that might not otherwise come up till months into the relationship; things like parenthood, marriage, finances, faith amidst trial, commitment to work, moral certainty under pressure, and more. If you choose your movies wisely, for more than entertainment value, looking for stories that have something useful to say about real life, you may just get the chance to ask some questions of your date that on their own would seem pushy, forced, or simply out of place. A good movie puts these issues on the table. If nothing good is playing, use books, news stories, sermons, music lyrics, holiday traditions, family pictures; the list of conversation starters is endless.

It's never shameful to want to know, in a dating relationship, where things have the potential of going. Of course, you'll want to bring things up tactfully, being realistic about where you are in your dating timeline; but to avoid the subject altogether, in this culture, is foolish.

Assess His Potential

Even the best test of character will be inconclusive. Why? Because you're dealing with young men, not fully mature grandfathers. In her article, "Faith for the Man He'll Become," Carolyn McCulley talks about the downside of knowing godly married men. Just as this generation expects to have all the material wealth now that it took their parents fifty years to accumulate, we expect young men to have the godly character of someone who has been married several decades. She writes,

There is a learning curve to a man's leadership as a husband and father. The qualities you can see in a fifty-year-old man's life were developed over fifty years.

There are twenty-five more years of growth ahead for the twenty-five-year-old man before it's fair to compare them. While you are called to be discerning about the characters of the men you befriend or court/date, you also have a part in encouraging these men to grow.[7]

You're not going to find 100 percent maturity before marriage, no matter how old the guy you're dating is. That's because it's not just the passage of time that seasons a man's character. The process of being married matures men if they stay committed. I've seen it in my own relationship with Steve. He's a much different man than the one I married ten years ago. He's more spiritually mature, more seasoned, even more handsome. But I'm different too. Hopefully, as you look at the single men you know with "eyes of faith," they're doing the same with you. Just as God uses marriage to mature the character of men, He uses it to redeem the nature of women. I'd venture to say I'm less harsh, more refined, and more feminine thanks to all the love, support, and encouragement Steve has poured into my life since we said, "I do."

What you're looking for is aptitude. No matter how old he is, he must have the ability to learn what it takes to be a husband and to grow in that role. Remember the SAT and ACT? They don't test you for college-level knowledge; they're assessing if you're ready to learn at that level. It's the same with dating. You're looking for the aptitude to make a commitment to marriage—the ability to step up and learn how to live out the vows of leadership, protection, and provision. And it's not just the men who benefit. In addition to looking at the single men you know for what they can become, don't forget that you're on the same path to maturity. All the more reason to journey together as man and wife.

Ask the Right Question

So you've met a man with good character and he's got a lot of potential in the future husband category. How do you know if he's "the one"? You've got to ask the right question.

In his article "Stop Test-Driving Your Girlfriend," pastor Michael Lawrence exposes the problem with that question.

[It's] not merely ironic. If what you're after is a marriage that will glorify God and produce real joy for you and your bride, it's also the *wrong* question. That's because the unstated goal of the question is "How do I know if she's the one . . . *for me*."

The question frames the entire decision-making process in fundamentally self-oriented—if not downright selfish—terms. And it puts the woman on an extended trial to determine whether or not she meets *your* needs, fits with *your* personality, and satisfies *your* desires. It places *you* at the center of the process, in the role of a window-shopper, or consumer at a buffet. In this scenario you remain unexamined, unquestioned, and unassailable—sovereign in your tastes and preferences and judgments.

The problem of course is that as a single Christian man, not only are you going to marry a sinner, but *you* are a sinner as well.[8]

Although the article is written for men, his point about the wrong question applies equally to women. Instead of asking if he's the right one, what you should be asking is, "Will [we] be able to serve God better together than apart?"

*E*ncourage His Spiritual Maturity

One of the most important things a young man should do to grow spiritually is seek out the wisdom of older men. Women aren't the only ones who need mentors. Titus 2 also speaks to young men. Paul instructs the older men "to be temperate, dignified, sensible, sound in faith, in love, in perseverance" so they can "urge the young men to be sensible; in all things show yourself to be an example of good deeds, with purity in doctrine, dignified, sound in speech which is beyond reproach, so that the opponent will be put to shame, having nothing bad to say about us" (vv. 2, 6–8 NASB). Even as you're praying for a mentor in your own life, pray for mentors for the young men you know.

How you encourage him is key. Trying to push, pull, or nag a guy into a pursuit of godliness is futile. Appealing to the leader in him has a profound way of influencing his behavior and decisions. That's how Abigail approached David, a man on a mission to kill her foolish husband, Nabal. She knew that such bloodshed would be devastating for David's calling and career. So she related to him as king, saying,

"When the Lord has done for my master every good thing
he promised concerning him and has appointed him leader
over Israel, my master will not have on his conscience the
staggering burden of needless bloodshed or of having
avenged himself. And when the Lord has brought my
master success, remember your servant."

(1 Samuel 25:30–31)

Her wisdom was greatly rewarded. Not only did David do an about-face, God struck the wicked Nabal dead, and Abigail became David's wife. (You can read the whole story in 1 Samuel 25.)

*D*REAM WITH HIM

God made men to need help. And he made women to give it. An essential part of helping is asking him about—and encouraging—his dreams. Ask him questions like, "If you could do any job and money wasn't an issue, what would you do?" "Of all the books you've read and movies you've seen, what's your favorite story? Why?" "What does it mean to you to take dominion?" Initially he may not know what to say. You may be the first person in his life to ever care about his secret aspirations. But keep asking. Likely, once he starts dreaming with you, he won't want to stop. But don't panic if he says he wants to be president, win the World Series, *and* build the next space station. It's not likely he'll actually do it all. He just needs permission to entertain the "ifs": If I could do anything, be anything, go anywhere, I would . . .

If you've encouraged him and he really doesn't know what he'd do given the opportunity, and he's perfectly content with where he is—especially if where he is happens to be is a part-time gig at the Pizza Hut—that's a red flag for the future. A man with no dreams, no higher aspirations, is less likely to be a suitable provider for his family. The goal, after all, is not just marriage, but a good one. You want a husband who's capable of maturing. You want a man who can grow with you into the fullness of all that God has for you as a couple.

If you have doubts in either direction—he's too pie-in-the-sky or he's down on being able to do anything more than he already has—that's a good thing to talk about with your mentor or mentor couple. A mature Christian friend will likely have the benefit of emotional detachment necessary to discern if he has what it takes to be a husband.

Steve and I spent a lot of our pre-dating, friendship time talking about our hopes and dreams for the future. We had so many shared interests and similar callings that it was natural to brainstorm where our passions might lead. We spurred each other on. All this before we were a couple. At one point before we started dating, Steve said, "Even if we live in different cities, we have to work together. We just have so much in common. I could see us meeting halfway every summer for joint family vacations!" I'm glad he realized it would be a lot easier if we just married each other (I'm not sure how our spouses would have felt about that shared vacation idea).

I think in the end our shared dreaming was what made Steve move from just friends to dating. Even before he felt romantic attraction, he felt the attraction of my admiration. There was something intoxicating to his masculine design about the way I believed in him. It meant so much to him he captured it in a poem he gave me alongside the *One Year Bible*.

Over a cup of coffee
Over a couple of months
Words laid on words
Prayers shared and delivered
Hearts woven
Minds triggered
A penetrating warm searching light
poured into dark abandoned places
Waking gently a great sleeper
Asking him not to forget his dreams

It's time to start asking.

Then Naomi said, "Wait, my daughter,
until you find out what happens.
For the man will not rest until
the matter is settled today."

RUTH 3:18

CHAPTER 7

Pulling a Ruth

ow that you know how to wake a sleeper, I have to
warn you that your belief and respect alone may not be
enough to move him to marriage. In fact, giving too
much, too soon may actually cause delays. Let me explain.

The first time I saw Steve I felt that little spark. It was during
opening week of classes at Regent University. A few days later,
we talked for the first time in the library. We were there for a
mandatory "how to use the library" tour, and to endure the
boredom, we started whispering about the books we were
reading. *He likes to read*, I thought. An immediate plus. I went
out a few days later and bought the book he mentioned just so
we'd have some guaranteed conversation.

Soon after, I noticed there was no newspaper or publication
for our school. So I suggested starting one. I invited several of
my new friends to a meeting at a local coffee shop. I mentioned
offhandedly to one that maybe he should bring Steve, knowing

that Steve had been the editor of his college yearbook. I hoped such a project would interest him.

We did start a publication—a Webzine, actually—at Steve's suggestion. It wasn't long before our team of five students was meeting weekly, working on a mission statement for our endeavor, *NeoPolitique* (*NP*), getting to know one another, and praying together for God's blessing on our efforts. It was a very nonthreatening way to get to know Steve better and a great chance to see him in his element: writing and editing and launching a new project. Of course, it didn't hurt that he had a chance to see my strengths too.

In the course of a few months, we became very good friends. In addition to all the *NP* meetings and outings, Steve and I found we had a lot in common and started doing things together, just the two of us. We'd go out for coffee or to a bookstore or to the movies. We spent a lot of time talking and learning more about one another. We weren't dating and the relationship was platonic. But I was hopeful.

During one memorable outing, we drove to Williamsburg, Virginia, for a day of retreating with the *NP* staff. Steve had some music he wanted me to hear, so I rode with him. *This is great,* I thought. *We'll have an hour to talk and be together, alone.* It couldn't have gone any better. We had a great time on the drive up and even seemed to be connecting in the midst of the larger group while sightseeing. I was beaming, thinking, *Surely he's getting it now. He must see the chemistry here.* As the day wound down, he even arranged for the same caravan partners on the ride home. Another hour alone. This was better than I expected.

We had only been in the car a few minutes when he dropped the bomb: "I've got to get back to school," he said. "Oh, really, why?" I asked.

"I've got a date with Kelli," he said.

A date? After our incredible time together today, you have the nerve to tell me you have a date with another woman? I was stunned.

Still, I was falling for him.

We spent the school year developing a deep friendship and by summer, we were spending time together every day. He was no longer dating anyone else (that Kelli thing fizzled out after a month or two), and everyone around us thought we were a couple. But I knew there was no agreement that we were anything more than pals. I was at my wits' end. Here was the man I wanted to marry, and he was oblivious to what a good match we were.

I was ready to put some of Mary Morken's advice to the test

*F*OLLOWING RUTH'S LEAD

Remember that retreat I mentioned where the Morkens talked about their own unlikely romance? After they finished, they took questions. Mary talked about why the times we live in make it so hard for marriages to form. I didn't waste a minute. "So what can we do about it?!" I asked.

She responded matter-of-factly: "Sometimes you have to 'pull a Ruth.'"

"What's that?" I asked.

Mary went on to tell us the story of Ruth. Set in the time of the judges—some of Israel's darkest days—Ruth left her homeland and her dead husband, and in a move of fierce loyalty and faith, headed to a foreign country with her mother-in-law, Naomi. Once there, she set about finding ways to provide food enough for herself and for Naomi. Her first day out, she happened upon the fields of Boaz, a "man of standing" and relative of Naomi's deceased husband.

According to Mary, Ruth's story of finding a husband in undesirable circumstances had a lot to teach us given our postmarriage culture. I was ready to follow Ruth's lead. Now all I needed was the modern-day application.

Prior to listening to Mary, I believed it was enough to "trust in the Lord with all my heart" and "seek first His kingdom." She assured me those things were fundamental, but didn't stop there. "Ruth lived in a stable society where families were involved in God's work of bringing mates together," Mary said. "The 'kinsman-redeemer' traditions helped a young widow marry again. In our day, we are in limbo without structures and social supports. We don't even know if potential mates believe in marriage the same as we do. Just how courtship should be done is up for grabs." Unlike Ruth, I didn't have a prescribed path to marriage. But I did have renewed hope that marriage could still happen in less-than-ideal circumstances. And now I had some help.

I had always heard the way to a man's heart was through his stomach, so I decided to host a dinner party where the guest list included Steve and the Morkens. Hu and Mary did a great job of asking questions that prompted us to think about where we were headed after graduation and whether we might journey together. And in the midst of the probing conversation, Steve was enjoying my chicken Italiano, baby greens, and homemade cheesecake.

The meal and conversation must have made the difference. After the Morkens left, Steve broached the subject of "us" for the very first time. Working together to clean up the dishes, he said it: "There's something between us, isn't there? The potential for more?" I was thrilled. Thrilled that he finally saw it and that he had the courage to acknowledge it. We spent the next hour talking about our friendship and all the reasons we would be such a good couple. He also talked about his doubts. About how I was different from the girls he had dated in the past. I guess I was the first Yankee to catch this Southern boy's fancy.

It wasn't a definitive conversation—he ended by saying, "I'm not sure where we go from here"—but it was the beginning.

And I was content to hope and pray like crazy.

Prayer played no small part in our budding romance. Since Steve had not yet made any commitment to me, I couldn't share the secrets of my heart with him—I had to rely on the Lord. My journals from those months of waiting were filled with prayers for patience and trust and ultimately, God's will. I knew that as much as I wanted Steve, I wanted even more to be in God's will. So I prayed that God's plan included Steve—and if it didn't, that He would change the desires of my heart.

Two and a half months passed after that conversation—still with no progress toward marriage or even an official transition to "dating." I was getting impatient. Steve was enjoying my encouragement—our shared dreaming—but maybe I was giving too many of the benefits without a commitment. It was time to act.

On our way to campus the morning before summer break was over, I laid it all on the line. "Steve, I want to get married and I hope it's to you. But if it's not, then we need to stop spending all this time together. Otherwise, no one else will ask me out—they all think we're dating." I said it in one breath, my heart pounding out of my chest. He was listening.

I knew it was an all-or-nothing proposition and that there was a good chance I'd walk away with nothing. But my desire really was marriage, and hanging out as buddies indefinitely wasn't going to get me any closer to that calling. I needed him to make it official; to be sure I wasn't wasting the most eligible days of my life on some endless holding pattern. "If you're not ready to state your intentions," I said, "then we have to stop spending all this time together."

I was asking him to lead. I was serious about being willing to walk away from our friendship, and he knew it. We agreed to spend the day apart and get back together that evening to talk.

Time moved a lot slower that day. I spent the hours thinking and praying, asking God to embolden Steve and open his heart to love. I knew with all of my being that we would be a good match. But I also knew that "palling around" wasn't getting me any closer to my desire for, and calling to, marriage. So I also prayed for my own strength to follow through if he said no.

What I was really doing was asking Steve to "chase the plane." I needed to know how he'd respond if forced to face life without me. It was like that classic scene from the movies. The one where you're rooting for the couple to get back on track after some kind of detour only to have one of the characters board a plane for a new chapter in life. Things look bleak. A tear rolls down the heroine's cheek as she stares out the window of the plane while it taxies down the runway. And that's when she sees him—out on the tarmac, chasing the plane. She can't hear him, but his lips appear to be saying, "Come back; I love you—I can't live without you."

OK, it's a little cheesy, but that's what Hollywood does best. And that vivid imagery can go a long way to help women in languishing relationships. What they need, more than anything, is to book a flight. At least figuratively. Even when women know their relationship is stalled or is headed in the wrong direction, they're often reluctant to do anything that might upset the status quo. They might think it's time to make the benefits of the relationship sweeter and hope he'll get it. More benefits aren't the answer. What a man who's stuck needs most is a sense of life without you. You have to get on your plane and be willing to take off, regardless of what he does.

Getting on your plane ends the "going-nowhere chapter." What comes next could be the "he chases the plane" chapter or maybe the "she meets her future husband on the plane" plot twist. You never know how the man in your life will respond. He might take a small step that proves to be in the right direction. He might exceed your expectations and ask you to marry him.

He might, unfortunately, prove he's not ready to be a husband. Whatever the outcome, you have to give him a chance to make the move.

Boarding the plane is your heroic step. The next heroic step is his. Don't take it for him. Don't ask the pilot to turn the plane around. Don't book a return flight as soon as you reach your destination. Don't obsess over the things you miss about him, or you'll find yourself right back where you started. Let him be the one who's motivated by missing you. It may lead to the best part of your story.

ℛETHINKING MY INTERPRETATION

Since I first started telling this story of how I "pulled a Ruth" on Steve, I've received hundreds of e-mails from women who want to know how they should apply what I said to their specific situations. Often the only similarity between their stories and mine is that they've got a crush on a longtime male friend. Each time I get a letter like that, I'm reminded of the heavy responsibility it is to suggest how certain biblical stories and attending principles apply to our lives. And each time I read one of those letters, I offer a quick prayer that I've rightly divided the word of truth (2 Timothy 2:15). I've also continued to read and study both the book of Ruth and the whole of Scripture, along with the writings of trusted biblical scholars, in order to increase my understanding.

What I've learned has significantly changed my ideas about the bold pursuit of a man.

Ruth's is not an ideal story—the norm we should strive for—but a story of redemption in difficult circumstances. Debbie Maken reminded me of that when I read her book, *Getting Serious about Getting Married*. In it she points out that the stories of Isaac and Rebekah, and Jacob and Rachel—not

Ruth—are the biblical norm for family formation. Unlike Ruth, those women had fathers and extended families who took an active part in helping them marry well and in a timely fashion. She writes,

> The Bible does include stories of women who didn't have a family agency working on their side, showing the vulnerability of flying solo. . . . Ruth's mother-in-law, Naomi, an elderly woman herself, hardly qualifies as an adequate covering with bargaining power because her idea of sending Ruth to the threshing room floor in the middle of the night was fraught with danger, physical harm, and costs to Ruth's reputation. . . . Ruth represents a widow in a rather exceptional situation. Rachel and Rebekah represent much more accurately what God intends for us through the protection of family and an active and negotiating father. . . . It's far better to be in the protected place of Rachel and Rebekah than in the perilous position of Ruth.[1]

When I first read Debbie's description, it made me bristle. I hadn't realized how undesirable Ruth's situation was, and it was a bit hard to accept. I guess I had brought a few too many modern sensibilities to my reading of the ancient story, wanting to make Ruth into one of the original examples of girl power. I was so inspired by the way she made good of a bad situation that I missed two key points: it would have been better had she been under the covering of a strong father figure, and she didn't "go after" just anyone.

Early in the story we learn that when Boaz arrived at the field where the gleaners were working, *he* noticed *her.* "Whose young woman is that?" he asked. When he found out that she was "the Moabitess who came back from Moab with Naomi," that she had asked to be allowed to glean with the poor, working diligently since morning "except for a short rest in the shelter," he was intrigued (Ruth 2:5–6).

But he didn't stop there. He actually singled her out saying,

"My daughter, listen to me. Don't go and glean in another field and don't go away from here. Stay here with my servant girls. Watch the field where the men are harvesting, and follow along after the girls. I have told the men not to touch you. And whenever you are thirsty, go and get a drink from the water jars the men have filled."

(RUTH 2:8–9)

Not only was it Boaz who initiated their first conversation, but what he said was significant. He was caring for her by providing for her physical needs for food and water as well as protecting her from harm at other, less honorable, men's hands.

Now it was Ruth's turn to respond. Ruth 2:10 says, "At this, she bowed down with her face to the ground. She exclaimed, 'Why have I found such favor in your eyes that you notice me—a foreigner?'"

At this point, we get a look at Ruth's character. Verses 11 and 12 say, "Boaz replied, 'I've been told all about what you have done for your mother-in-law since the death of your husband— how you left your father and mother and your homeland and came to live with a people you did not know before. May the Lord repay you for what you have done. May you be richly rewarded by the Lord, the God of Israel, under whose wings you have come to take refuge.'"

Ruth's integrity preceded her. Such that Boaz didn't just give her choice gleanings, water, and protection; but he also blessed her. No small thing in Israelite culture. Then, in a public gesture of provision, Boaz included Ruth in the afternoon meal, offering her bread and wine vinegar. She was the only one among the gleaners—those in poverty and foreigners who were permitted to pick up what was left behind in the fields—who was part of the mealtime invitation.

Later, when Ruth relayed the day's events to her mother-in-law, sharing with her leftover bread from the meal and an abundance of grain, Naomi immediately recognized the high character of Boaz and his potential as a husband for Ruth. "Where did you glean today? Where did you work? Blessed be the man who took notice of you!" she exclaimed (2:19). Boaz was already husbanding Ruth, and Naomi recognized it. Contrary to what I originally thought about this story, Naomi was not encouraging Ruth to "go after" Boaz in a modern-day-type pursuit. She was guiding Ruth to respond to what Boaz had already initiated. By the time Naomi told Ruth about the kinsman-redeemer system and asked her to go to Boaz at the threshing floor, she had every reason to believe Boaz would respond positively. Naomi said with confidence, "[He] will not rest until the matter is settled" (3:18). How could she know this? Because she had evidence of his character.

This is no small oversight. In order to "pull a Ruth," you have to be dealing with a Boaz. And with Steve, I was. He had already demonstrated much about his high character through the course of our friendship. I knew that he was honest and hardworking, that he was a strong believer with mature faith and that our goals, passions, and convictions were well-aligned. I also knew that he believed in and wanted marriage and children. What I didn't know was if he could see himself married to me.

When it came time for my ultimatum ("call this what it is, or no more access to me"), I said what I did so that we could end the going-nowhere chapter of our friendship. I knew in doing so that I risked ending our whole story, but it was time to put his character to the test. I needed to see if, like Boaz, he would "settle the matter" today.

After spending the day apart praying, Steve picked me up after dinner, and we went for a walk at dusk around a small lake on campus. When we finished the circle and sat down on a bench, my hands were trembling. I couldn't guess what he would say. He wasn't giving me any hints. I remember the intensity in his eyes when he started talking. "Candice, what we have is obviously more than friendship. I'm sorry it's taken me so long to say it, but now I'm ready to say we're dating."

God answered my prayers that day. Steve opened his heart, and with the advice of the Morkens, he "let love grow" between us. It was a little awkward going from platonic to romantic, but the Morkens were there with advice and wisdom to mentor us through the process.

It was a wonderful day of celebration when, six months later, Steve got down on one knee in a small garden in Williamsburg, Virginia, and asked me to be his wife. Then it was my turn to say yes.

*The secret of success is
consistency of purpose.*

BENJAMIN DISRAELI

CHAPTER 8

Living like you're planning to marry

It was March Madness and in a rare moment of not much to do, Steve turned on the college basketball play-offs. I was doing something much more exciting—balancing our checkbook—when I overheard a Charles Schwab commercial. It ended with a pointed question: "Are you planning to retire, or just hoping to?" You may not be thinking much about retirement, but try replacing the word *retire* with *marry*.

"Are you planning to marry, or just hoping to?"

Many women grow up hoping they'll get married someday. Hope is good. It's what keeps you going when you're weary (Isaiah 40:30–31). It's what sustains you when marriage seems out of reach. But hope alone isn't enough. You have to live like you're planning to marry.

So what does that look like? Does it mean loading up your day planner with strategies and to-do items for getting married by Christmas? YES! And a whole lot more. OK, not really. That would be both unromantic and inconsistent with a Christian woman's approach. When I hear the phrase, "living like you're planning to marry," I think of "planning" in the context of "intending." *Intending* means doing things that are consistent with what you expect to happen and avoiding things that aren't. When it comes to getting married, intending looks a lot like basic Christian discipleship—doing the things God calls you to do and not doing the things He tells you to avoid.

Don't worry; I'm not suggesting if you just try to be a better Christian, God will reward you with a husband. It's not like "good Christians" get husbands and "bad ones" don't. This isn't a cosmic rewards plan with God pulling a husband from his prize box for the women who do everything on His checklist. It's simply, elegantly, the unfolding of sowing and reaping.

Paul wrote, "Do not be deceived: God cannot be mocked. A man reaps what he sows" (Galatians 6:7). Good living produces good fruit. Bad living produces bad fruit. "What about forgiveness?" you ask. "Can't God still bring a husband to someone who has messed up a lot?" God does forgive us again and again. But Paul encourages us not to go on sinning just because grace abounds. We shouldn't presume upon God by doing whatever we please while hoping He'll still bless us with a husband. That's not a good plan for marriage any more than declaring bankruptcy is a good plan for financial health.

SOWING AND REAPING

If the things God requires of us as Christian disciples, many also facilitate good marriages. Take just two examples: community and stewardship. Marriage shouldn't be your chief reason for doing these things, but it has the potential to grow among the good fruit that results from righteous living.

LIFE IN THE BODY

When Mary Morken discussed the challenges singles face in our culture, she encouraged us saying, "Talk about marriage. Don't be afraid of the subject. You are young, godly men and women; you should want to be married and be willing to do the work to get there." She explained that the mere fact of our conversations could lead to good matches. "Stand in the gap for each other," she said. "Facilitate the courtship process and through self-disclosure, express your beliefs about marriage and courtship within your group of friends. You never know; that group may include your future mate." We were all a little shocked by her boldness and unconventional approach. We also knew we weren't finding any success doing things our way.

That kind of pointed advice from an older believer was what I needed: both the practical suggestions for what I talked about with my friends, as well as the practice of getting input from a mentor. For me it was a new way of experiencing the benefits of Christian community.

Community. We say we want it and talk about how much we've lost it, but true and vibrant Christian community eludes many of us. Blame it on the tension between the community God calls us to and the values of individualism and consumerism we esteem so much in American culture. Reading the writings of Paul, Peter, and James about what it means to be the body (see 1 Corinthians 12:22–26; James 2:1–4; 1 Peter 4:8–10), you realize just how countercultural it really is. Christian community is much more than having a hundred "friends" on a social networking site or hanging out with buddies from college and work.

Biblical community requires thinking of others before ourselves, serving others sacrificially, and allowing others to need and depend on us. It also includes an aspect of diversity even more intense than any utopian university celebration—with people of all races, ages, economic status, degrees of health, and social standing living in fellowship. It includes honor for gray hair and a strong emphasis on younger men and women learning from those with more wisdom and experience.

I have to be honest. As I discover more of what God calls us to in community, my first thought is, *Whoa, I need some boundaries here.* But without deep, intergenerational, other-centered community, we flounder in isolation. No one can interfere with our lives, but no one is there to help us either. When we choose to live outside an engaged community of mutual service, we have no choice but to fend for ourselves.

As in so many areas of Christian discipleship, however, it's at the point of discomfort and inability to understand the purpose behind God's ways that we begin to see the fruit of obedience. As we surrender our independence and our standards of who is "worthy" of our relational investment, we start to experience the blessings of living in the body. We see what it means for iron to sharpen iron. We experience the comfort of bearing one another's burdens. We get a glimpse of the fellowship that awaits us in heaven.

This may sound idealistic given the imperfections of Christians and of the churches we've attended. But no one said living in the body wouldn't be awkward or without disappointments. And you have more to gain by growing in relationship with the larger body of believers than you do if you're limited to yourself or even a group of peers who are all in the same boat.

Though it's not the primary reason we live in Christian community, it's no less true that this is the environment in which we are most likely to meet a man pursuing a godly wife. As I mentioned in "You Need a Network," community provides the framework for receiving the protection, input, accountability, and encouragement essential for a strong foundation for marriage.

What does your community look like? Are you in fellowship with a multigenerational body of believers who encourage and challenge each other? Are there people in your life who are able to see your Christian character in action and also know you desire a good marriage?

I ask this last question because I believe there is a great untapped social network among older women that rivals in quality the connections of any online social network. In "Waking a Great Sleeper," I talked about the large number of Christian bachelors. The problem is, many aren't plugged into a local church while they're pursuing their education, building their careers, or traveling. Others are the kind who slip in to church late and leave early or who "worship" out on a mountain somewhere. That makes them harder to find. But not impossible. There is a group of people who know where these men are. They are the moms, aunts, grandmothers, Sunday school teachers, and neighbors who have known them since they were little boys. They may still have their pictures on their refrigerators. Some of these women pray for these men every day—asking God to protect them and bless them with prudent wives.

This network that was once the source of many good matches (and mentoring support) has diminished over the years as single women spend most of their time with peers. I've also noticed high-profile Christian singles telling older women to stop asking them about their dating life and stop trying to set them up on blind dates. It's true those questions can feel intrusive and some blind dates are disastrous, but why write off their help entirely? It's counterproductive to give older women—who may have good leads—the impression that you can take care of yourself, and that any effort to help is interfering.

I'm not suggesting you go crash the next church potluck and corner these women in search of their little black books.

It's my experience, however, that women who participate in vibrant, multigenerational Christian community are more likely to benefit from this network. If you seek first the kingdom of God in your pursuit of community, the opportunity for a good marriage is one of the many things that God can add to your life (Matthew 6:33).

AN LOAN FROM GOD

In addition to community, the other area of discipleship that can lead to marriage is stewardship. For some, "stewardship" implies just being smart with your money—knowing when to make a good investment so you can get a good return. But it's more than that. To get the full context, you have to go back to the definition of *steward*: someone who cares for the belongings of another. It's sobering to think how God trusts us when He asks us to be stewards of anything. He generously gives us talents, money, time, relationships, our bodies, and more and says, "This is all from Me; now use it for My glory" (see James 1:17, 1 Corinthians 10:31).

The idea of God handing us all these resources and then asking for a return on His investment is an affront to our consumer culture that says, "It's your money; spend it however you want. No one can tell you what to do with your time; go wherever you want and do whatever looks interesting. That's your body; don't let anyone dictate how you use it. Those are your talents; leverage them to make as much money as you can. Your relationships are your business; do whatever feels good."

Such is the tension of our age. Sadly, many of us have learned to be better consumers than stewards. We've had more practice learning how to get all the stuff marketers promise will make life richer than we've had practice testing God's principles that promise true abundant life.

Like the steward with one talent, many of us have little to show for what God has entrusted to us. His expectations have minimal impact on our checkbooks, our calendars, our media consumption, or our bodies. Yet the truth of those principles endures throughout time. He still calls us to view our bodies as temples of the Holy Spirit, and He reminds us, "that those who have been given a trust must prove faithful" (1 Corinthians 4:2).

The fruit of good stewardship is "enoughness." We learn not to be anxious about our lives, what we will eat, drink, or wear (Matthew 6:25). We learn to be content (Hebrews 13:5). But freedom from worry isn't the only benefit. As you faithfully use your gifts and passion to serve needs where they emerge (Romans 12:3–8), you can experience right now the elusive sense of purpose and fulfillment so many singles seek (Ephesians 2:10). And of great interest to readers of this book, stewardship puts you in a better position to marry well.

The more you embrace the fact that your money, time, body—every good thing you have—ultimately is not your own, the better prepared you'll be to become one in every way with your spouse. This, it turns out, is one of the struggles researchers suspect leads to lower satisfaction in later marriages. People who marry after a long season of singleness find it more difficult to merge their finances, schedules, and other aspects of their structured routines. In fact, it shouldn't be a surprise that more couples are keeping separate checking accounts after they marry, and some builders even see a trend in couples requesting separate bedrooms.[1]

The harder you work to reject the lifestyle of debt, the more ready you'll be to marry and start a family. In 1997, when the rate of debt was even lower than it is now,[2] outstanding loans were already having a negative effect on marriage rates. A survey conducted that year by Nellie Mae, the largest nonprofit provider of student loans, found 15 percent of graduates were delaying getting married because of education debt.

And today, says sociologist Allan Carlson, "By taking on the debt from Guaranteed Student Loans, young adults are delaying marriage and pushing back childbearing for a decade or more."[3] Dr. Morken introduced Steve and me to the expression "clear decks." "When your decks are clear," he said, "you're ready for opportunities." You don't have to work through a lot of complications in order to make the financial merger that is a marriage. But that's exactly what's happening with lots of couples —especially those who have spent a long time being single.[4]

Steve and I didn't put marriage off because of our debt, but we definitely started at a disadvantage. We joke that our wedding vows could have been, "I, Visa, take thee, student loan. . ." We weren't wise with our money (we still kick ourselves for the lattes we financed), and it created challenges we could have avoided if we'd been faithful. Not only did we have a hole to dig out of, but also the mentality we were in at the time became the pattern we continued—acting like debt was a normal part of our marriage. It's so much better when couples start out financially free.

BAD SEED, BAD ENDS

We can trust that when we plant good seed in the areas of community and stewardship, God will provide us with a good crop. That's how the world He created works. Still, many women sow bad seed, then pray for good fruit. It's like spending time with friends instead of studying for a test and then asking God to help you pass. We do it in many areas of life, but perhaps most obviously in the area of sex.

We've all heard that sex before marriage is wrong. Ephesians 5:3 says it unequivocally, "But among you there must not be even a hint of sexual immorality, or of any kind of impurity, or of greed, because these are improper for God's holy people." Instead of taking that moral warning to heart and fleeing temptation, we too often adopt the approach our culture has taught all too well—trying to separate the pleasures of forbidden fruit from their bitter aftertaste.

Consequence management. That's how we view sex—it's why there's so much emphasis on avoiding pregnancy and preventing STDs. But condoms can't protect your heart. And they can't protect your future marriage either. Couples justify sex before marriage with any number of reasons: "We're going to get married anyway;" "we're already married in our hearts;" "we didn't mean to let it happen;" "we want to make sure we're sexually compatible." Whatever their rationale, one thing's certain: premarital sex reinforces in their minds that marriage is no boundary for sex. And the divorce rate confirms it: for every sexual partner you have before marriage, your chance for divorce goes up.[5]

I used to think the primary harm of premarital sex to future marriages was the entanglement of previous partners. In candid conversations, however, friends have told me how much hurt and disappointment can come just from the sexual liberties they took with the person they ended up marrying. Michael Lawrence, associate pastor of Capitol Hill Baptist Church, says, "I don't know any couple who wishes they were more sexually active before they got married."

STICKING TOGETHER OR STUCK?

It may sound unconventional, but one of the worst things about premarital sex is that the couple eventually gets married. Don't misunderstand; couples who have had sex need to seriously consider marriage. They should ask, "Can we make a good marriage?" The problem is those couples are in a bad position to objectively answer that question. Something stronger than their minds is in charge. The chemical bonding God designed sex to produce has begun its work, and two people who are still in the process of determining if they are a good fit find themselves being welded together.

In an interview with Scott Stanley, codirector of the Center for Marital and Family Studies, he likened a sexual relationship to a pot boiling over on the stove. Sexually active couples can't see what's in the pot of their relationship for all the steam, foam, and bubbles. Is it nourishing porridge? Is it even edible? They can't tell because sex—like heat to a pot—obscures what's really in there. Instead of enhancing their relationship, illicit sex dictates it, leaving them disoriented and ill-equipped to make healthy decisions. He says the only way to see what you have in the pot—if it's a good relationship able to go the distance or a stinker that shouldn't continue—is to turn off the heat.

In his research, Dr. Stanley discovered commitment has two distinct aspects: sticking together—the choice to be loyal—and being stuck together—the reality of intertwining your life with another person in a way that makes it hard to leave. Though being stuck is a vital restraint for spouses who are tempted to leave in a moment of disappointment, it's bad glue for a couple who hasn't determined if they want to be so entwined.

In Stanley's research on cohabiting couples, he found that the restraints of a shared apartment, furniture, and in tragic cases, babies born out of wedlock, were enough to keep women in relationships they otherwise might have abandoned. Not-so-great relationships developed an inertia that kept them moving forward, all the way to marriage. The result: marriages with below-average satisfaction.

This is true not only for couples who live together, but also for couples who live apart but are sexually active (especially if they end up spending a lot of time at each other's places). When

I watch couples who are obviously a bad fit struggle to break up, I'm not surprised to learn they are having sex.

✐ HY MEN NEED SEX

I recognize there are two categories of readers—those who have had sex and those who haven't. Among those who have had sex, some are repentant and others aren't. Among those who haven't had sex are those who have been tested with opportunities for it and those who haven't. Whatever your sexual history, the goal remains: Live from today forward like you're planning to marry—like you're planning to one day fully enjoy the blessings of sex within a good marriage. For those who have had sex already, true repentance—admitting your sin and turning away—allows you to experience God's gracious forgiveness and restoration.

Premarital sexual activity is incompatible with Christian discipleship. Perseverance in purity is central to it. It's also central to your path to marriage. As Sarah Hinlicky wrote in "Subversive Virginity," "A virgin woman is an unattainable object of desire, and it is precisely her unattainability that increases her desirability."[6] This applies both to those who've never had sex as well as those who've repented and gone back to being chaste; what's often called "secondary virginity."

Men need the motivation that the promise of sex provides, and women need the security of marriage to fully embrace it. "Not having sex before marriage is a way of insisting that the most interesting part of your life will take place *after* marriage," writes Wendy Shalit in *A Return to Modesty*, "and if it's more interesting, maybe then it will last. And . . . if it lasts, maybe then you can finally be safe."[7]

Men don't see marriage, or anticipate it, the way women do. When the benefits of marriage are doled out prematurely, from their perspective, all that remains are the responsibilities. You're thinking, *Marriage will be all this, plus*—plus we can set up a home, plus we can have kids together, plus we can grow old together, and more. He's thinking, *Marriage will be all this, minus*—minus my freedom, minus my financial independence, minus my old friends, etc. And so you have the tired old cliché about the cow and the free milk.

The full context of our sexual drive and its purposes is much more significant than we can comprehend in a moment of temptation in a dimly lit room. Dr. James Dobson goes so far as to say that energy that holds people together is sexual in nature. In his book *Romantic Love* he writes:

The physical attraction between men and women causes them to establish a family and invest themselves in its development. It encourages them to work and save and toil to ensure the survival of their families. Their sexual energy provides the impetus for the raising of healthy children and for the transfer of values from one generation to the next.

Sexual drives urge a man to work when he would rather play. They cause a woman to save when she would rather spend. In short, the sexual aspect of our nature—when released exclusively within the family— produces stability and responsibility that would not otherwise occur. When a nation is composed of millions of devoted, responsible family units, the entire society is stable, responsible and resilient.

If sexual energy within the family is the key to a healthy society, then its release outside those boundaries is potentially catastrophic. The very force that binds a people together then becomes the agent for its own destruction.[8]

Living a life of purity is a tremendous challenge in the midst of our hypersexualized culture. But it's nowhere as challenging as trying to manage all the seen and unseen consequences that come when we reject God's design. Worse still is trying to grow a good marriage in a garden filled with the weeds you've planted. It's well worth the effort to stay pure, or if you've already fallen, to repent, receive forgiveness, and be pure again.

SEIZING OPPORTUNITIES

While there is much we can do to sow good seeds and avoid sowing bad seeds, there is one essential aspect of marrying well we can't control—the opportunities that come our way. That's why it's so important to seize those that do. A woman who's living like she's planning to marry will recognize four threats to good opportunities: procrastinating, aiming too high, hyperindependence, and avoiding risk.

PROCRASTINATING

In her book *What Our Mothers Didn't Tell Us*, Danielle Crittenden compares the social life of young women to a train station.

~~~~~~

> When a woman is young and reasonably attractive, men will pass through her life with the regularity of subway trains; even when the platform is empty, she'll expect another to be coming along soon. . . . But if a woman remains single until her age creeps up past thirty, she may find herself tapping at her watch and staring down the now mysteriously empty tunnel, wondering if there hasn't been a derailment or accident somewhere along the line. When a train does finally pull in, it is filled with misfits and crazy men. . . . The sensible, decent,

not-bad-looking men a woman rejected at twenty-four because she wasn't ready to settle down all seem to have gotten off at other stations.[9]

It's not always that bad, but to remain ignorant of the possibility that it could be is perilous. I've heard from readers at *boundless.org* who say they wish they could go back and redo their early twenties. Many bemoan wasted opportunities to marry when they were just starting to build their careers; others agree that now that they're in their thirties, the pickings are thin. One said she didn't realize till she was still single at thirty just what a good proposal she'd had when she was a young twentysomething. As is common, that good guy is married now, to someone else.

For those women who haven't had many—or any—dates, even in their twenties, being reminded that it gets harder to marry well the older you get is not meant to discourage, but to show that intentionality is more important than ever. The sooner you start, the better.

"You have people waiting to marry later and later," Dr. Stanley told me in an interview for *Boundless*. "But the risk of marrying young, which has been very clear and strong, is really pretty much gone by twenty-two. The risk doesn't keep going down with age. And other risks accumulate during that period. During that time people are greatly increasing the complexity of their lives in terms of finances and sexual relationships and then when people finally do enter marriage, there's all this history, which is very relevant to the risks in the marriage." [10]

God designed us with a prime time for marrying and having babies. That may be controversial, but it's indisputable: Our biology, fertility, sexuality, energy, and beauty all reinforce that we have a window of opportunity to form a family well. This is not to say that if you're past a certain age, God can't bless you, but there is a season when some things—especially children—are more likely. Tragically, in our current culture, many women don't realize it until their window starts to close.

AIMING TOO HIGH

Jane Austen's novels are full of endearing characters who are continually checking their expectations against the reality of what is in front of them. They want romance, but they temper that desire with what they know they need—a provider and protector—as well as with the offers they could reasonably command.

Unlike Elizabeth Bennett, Charlotte Lucas, and Elinor Dashwood, women today have an unprecedented number of choices in every category. How they spend their lives is largely a matter of preference and whim. And while having no choices makes life "almost unbearable," says Barry Schwartz, author of *The Paradox of Choice*, "as the number of choices keeps growing, negative aspects of having a multitude of options begin to appear. As the number of choices grows further, the negatives escalate until we become overloaded. At this point, choice no longer liberates, but debilitates. It might even be said to tyrannize." The plethora of choices affects even relationships, says Schwartz. "A range of life choices has been available to Americans for quite some time. But in the past, the 'default' options were so powerful and dominant that few perceived themselves to be making choices. Whom we married was a matter of choice, but we knew that we would do it as soon as we could and have children, because that was something all people did. . . . Today, all romantic possibilities are on the table; all choices are real. Which is another explosion of freedom, but which is also another set of choices to occupy our attention and fuel our anxieties."[11]

For better and worse, we've made great strides since Jane

Austen's day. We're an accomplished generation. Barbara Dafoe Whitehead says today's single women are "able to achieve something that even powerful women in the past fell short of: an independence that rests largely or completely on [their] own accomplishments as well as [their] own resources. . . . They've been on a strenuous path to achievement since girlhood. Today's single women are like specimen orchids. They've been bred to win prizes."[12] But all this prep and training for super-achievement comes with a downside. We have few remaining practical needs for a man. We don't need his money, his house, even his name. We can take self-defense classes and learn how to shoot a handgun so his brawn isn't as essential as it once was either. Ironically, when you don't *need* a man, your expectations for what a husband should be go up. We've lost our perspective of what a reasonable opportunity for marriage is.

Providing a good home, putting food on the table, taking out intruders, and siring children he could do. At least most men could. But living up to your wildest romantic fantasies, being your lifelong soul mate, anticipating all your deepest longings and desires, and feeling with you as deeply as Oprah does, well, that's a tall order for someone designed by God to be a husband. We may think what we want is a male version of us, but that's not what God designed men to be.

"The centuries-old ideal of friendship in marriage, or what sociologists call companionate marriage, may be evolving into a more exalted and demanding standard of a spiritualized union of souls," says David Popenoe, codirector of the National Marriage Project.[13] It's no small number of singles waiting for soul mate perfection. Ninety-four percent of never-married twentysomethings think that when they marry, their spouse should be their soul mate first and foremost.[14]

"Nothing has produced more unhappiness than the concept of a soul mate," said psychiatrist Frank Pittman in *Psychology*

Today. He and several other marriage experts are concerned that the growing expectation for a perfect match is frustrating singles needlessly and threatening their chances of a satisfying marriage. What they're looking for, says the author of the article, is "the man or woman who will counter our weaknesses, amplify our strengths and provide the unflagging support and respect that is the essence of a contemporary relationship."[15] Popenoe and Whitehead call such marriages "SuperRelationships." They report that "marriage is losing much of its broad public and institutional character," becoming instead "an intensely private spiritualized union, combining sexual fidelity, romantic love, emotional intimacy, and togetherness. . . . [it's] emotionally deep but socially shallow."[16]

Of course, we all want to be known fully and still loved deeply. But if you're holding out for someone who loves you just as you are and who will never ask you to change, you're setting yourself up for failure. What happens when you encounter the inevitable turbulence of marriage? You may doubt you've found your mystical soul mate, after all. Human relationships will always be flawed because we're all fallen. To expect otherwise is a precursor to divorce.

Despite fantasies of marriage as an endless date, a lifelong partnership is actually about thriving in the day-to-day stuff of life: paying the bills, cleaning the house, raising the kids. A lasting marriage requires commitment, no matter what. You have to go into it expecting highs *and* lows. Of course, every life has lows. A good marriage, however, makes the lows a lot more bearable. If "into every life a little rain must fall," how much better to have someone helping you hold the umbrella.

As you release flawed soul mate expectations in favor of biblical ones, you may start to see opportunities you didn't notice before. Think that's "settling"? I'm not saying you should lower your expectations; I am saying you should realign them.

A lot of women have good friends who are men. "Oh, we're just friends. We'd never think of dating," they say about them. "We're not romantic." Why not? Too often we overlook men in the "just friends" category because we're not attracted to them. I remember the "looks conversation" I had more than once with my mom. "Oh, he is so cute," I'd say. "Mom, you have to admit it. Isn't he cute?" "He's OK, honey. Just remember, looks aren't everything." There are worse things in life than marrying an unattractive man.

Back when parents chose their daughters' husbands for them, they noticed physical appearance very little. They knew externals played a minor role, if any, in creating a healthy family. I'm not suggesting a return to the days of arranged marriages— they had problems of their own—but we can borrow a principle from them: if a woman is paired with an upstanding man, love may blossom.

Why not try that approach? Instead of asking, *To whom am I attracted?* start asking, *Of my male friends, who would be a godly husband, strong partner, and good father?* Thinking of men this way, you might be surprised who captures your heart. Attraction isn't static. A man whose looks initially don't catch your eye may become a visual feast once you get to know his heart, his character, his personality. A face is just wrapping paper. You'd be a fool on Christmas day to discard gifts that had too much tape or reused bows, before you even looked to see what was inside. Sometimes the tackiest wrapping covers the best gift.

Steve looked different than the man I imagined I'd marry. When I first saw him I thought he was nice looking, but what really captured me was *him*. His interests, his calling, his passion, his humor. All of him. And as we grew in friendship, I grew more attracted to his looks. (I know he'd say the same about me.)

*H*YPERINDEPENDENCE

Once you've realigned your expectations, you'll be in a great place to start acting on good opportunities. But a godly man who's pursuing you for marriage isn't enough. Now you've got to ask yourself, Are you ready to fit in with him?

I've received lots of comments from women who spent their twenties hoping for marriage, only to find that when a proposal finally happened in their thirties, it wasn't as appealing as they'd always assumed it would be. Suddenly their long-held desire for marriage was challenged by their equally strong satisfaction with their way of life. While single, they thought they were merely biding time. In reality, they were establishing a lifestyle that, should the time come, would be hard to give up. Living like you're planning to marry requires that you not overdo independence.

Even women who deeply desire marriage find themselves pouring themselves into their life as a single woman with little thought or planning for their future as a married one. They're hard at work on their careers and financial goals—their "Plan B" as many call it—just in case Plan A is delayed or never happens. It's understandable, and in our culture, praised, to make the most of your singleness. The problem is that Plan A requires moving toward oneness—interdependence—with another person in marriage. Plan B finds you becoming increasingly independent so you don't need another person. It's easy to see how actively investing in B could undermine A.

Part of this trend flows from a fear that men aren't trustworthy; that they'll inevitably let women down. Many women have heard as much from their own mothers. This expectation often drives women to invest more in Plan B than Plan A. But as a wise friend told me, "When Plan B gets all the attention, it becomes Plan A."

That's not to say you should sit around idly, waiting for a good man to show up. Talented women should use their talents. But to believe without exception that "life doesn't begin after marriage" can actually prevent marriage from happening. Some things in life should be delayed, most obviously having sex and getting pregnant. There are lots of things we put on hold or don't do because they're counterproductive to other things we want more. (Saying no to a party so you can study for finals, avoiding a great sale on jeans because you're saving for a car, waiting to see a movie until you've read the book—these are just a few examples that come to mind.) Why should it be any different with our desire for marriage? Delaying gratification in some cases is worth it; the object of desire is often sweeter when you wait for it till the appropriate time.

Even as you pursue your interests and develop your talents, it's important to keep in mind that the drive for independence on the one hand can undermine the longing for interdependence of an intimate partnership on the other.

One thing's certain—getting married is getting harder. That's due in part to our culture's lack of expectations and encouragement to marry. And for women, it's due in large part to the lack of initiative on the part of men. But let's not forget that one main reason single women stay single is that in many cases, they make decisions that make it less likely they will be prepared to marry should the opportunity arise.

Danielle Crittenden talks about the truth that betrays "the supposedly happy, autonomous life" of the single woman. "Once you have ceased being single, you suddenly discover that all that energy you spent propelling yourself toward an independent existence was only going to be useful if you were planning to spend the rest of your life as a nun or a philosopher on a mountaintop . . . In preparation for a life spent with someone else, however, it was not going to be helpful." [17]

There are things that as a single woman you'll have to do on your own. But that doesn't mean you have to mimic the world's way. You can prepare for the interdependence marriage will require.

AVOIDING RISK

What if you do everything I've suggested and marriage doesn't happen right away? Are you willing to leave behind the safety of your independent routine to risk trying? Will you become interdependent with someone who will inevitably let you down? It's tempting to wait until there is no risk, until there's no chance you could be hurt. Or hurt again. Your fears are real, but you can't let them have the last word. To live like you're planning to marry is risky because love is risky. C. S. Lewis describes it in vivid terms.

There is no safe investment. To love at all is to be vulnerable. Love anything, and your heart will certainly be wrung and possibly be broken. If you want to make sure of keeping it intact, you must give your heart to no one, not even to an animal. Wrap it carefully round with hobbies and little luxuries; avoid all entanglements; lock it up safe in the casket or coffin of your selfishness. But in that casket—safe, dark, motionless, airless—it will change. It will not be broken; it will become unbreakable, impenetrable, irredeemable.[18]

I doubt you'd really want to live where there's no risk of hurt.

What opportunities might be masked by procrastinating, aiming too high, hyperindependence, or avoiding risk? Living like you're planning to marry means intentionally resisting these cultural traps and instead cultivating community, stewardship, and purity—the elements of Christian discipleship that can best help you recognize and embrace opportunities.

So, are you planning to marry or just hoping to? Isn't it time to connect the two?

In the film *Facing the Giants*, the lead character, a downcast, losing high school football coach who's questioning everything about his life, finds encouragement in the story of two farmers.

"There were two farmers who desperately needed rain," his friend tells him. "And both of them prayed for rain. But only one of them went out to prepare his fields to receive it.

"Which one do you think trusted God to send the rain?"

"The one who prepared his fields for it."

"Which one are you? God will send the rain when He's ready. You need to prepare your field to receive it."[19]

Dream no small dreams, for they have
no power to move the hearts of men.

ATTRIBUTED TO
JOHANN WOLFGANG VON GOETHE

CHAPTER 9

Pray boldly

Now that you know some of the ways God works through means, the roles reserved for key people in your life, and the things you can do to help marriage happen, let's go back to what I used to think was the *only* avenue to marriage: prayer.

It's one thing to pray for a husband. I suspect every never-married woman has done that in moments of desperation. But what would it look like to pray boldly, fervently, ceaselessly? And how would that kind of prayer affect the outcome?

HAVE FAITH

When I was single, I used to pray for a husband like this,

Oh, God, please don't make me be single my whole life. I really want to be married. Oh, I hope it's not Your will for me to be single. I don't think I could do it! Please

bring someone into my life soon, very soon. But help me
to be patient in the meantime. And God, if You do want
me to be single—but I hope You don't—please give me the
grace for it, because I really don't feel it. Did I mention
how much I hope that's not Your will for me?

I wish I had read about Bartimaeus back then. It wasn't until after I was married that his story, recorded in Mark 10:46–52, leapt off the page.

When Bartimaeus, the blind beggar, heard that Jesus was approaching, he shouted, "Jesus, Son of David, have mercy on me!" The exclamation point emphasizes his volume. In a book known for economy of words and punctuation, it's clear this was no tepid request. Even as the crowd rebuked him, telling him to be quiet, the Bible says, "He shouted all the more, 'Son of David, have mercy on me!'"

His clamor was rewarded. When Jesus asked Bartimaeus, "What do you want me to do for you?" he replied, "Rabbi, I want to see." He was frank about what he wanted and fully expected healing, for he knew Jesus had the authority to do it. By acknowledging Him as, "Jesus, Son of David," Bartimaeus was in essence saying he believed Jesus was Messiah and King.[1]

Jesus didn't disappoint. "Immediately he received his sight," the Bible reports. But it wasn't Bartimaeus's flattery, neediness, or even his volume that made the difference. As Jesus said, "Your faith has healed you."

LEARNING TO REALLY PRAY

Unlike Bartimaeus, I asked, but doubted. It's not that I disbelieved God *could* bring me a mate—I just didn't think He *would*. Still my heart longed to be married. And on it went. Till Mary Morken helped me see my prayers for what they were: faithless requests for something I wasn't even sure it was OK to want. I was embarrassed to admit my desire for marriage, and here she was encouraging me to not only acknowledge my hopes, but also pursue them.

Suddenly I felt free to really pray. My petitions changed. No longer weighed down by doubts that what I wanted was good, I asked with confidence:

Lord, You created me. And I believe You created marriage for my good and Your glory. I don't know Your timeline, but I'm asking You to fulfill my desire to be married.

Then I thanked Him for what I believed He would do:

Thank You, Lord, for this strong desire You've placed in my heart. Thank You that You've already been where I'm headed and that You know what my future holds. Thank You for marriage and for my future mate. Please be with him and prepare his heart to do Your will.

Once I started praying this way, things started happening.

FEAR OF FATHERS

Just knowing it's OK to pray boldly may not be enough. Many women have to start by overcoming their fear of their earthly fathers. Depending on how your dad responded when you asked him for things as a child, asking God for a husband may feel too risky. If you repeatedly heard "no" or suffered abuse or neglect at your dad's hands—even when what you asked for was good—you may be afraid to try again.

No matter what your earthly father is like—even if he gave you more stones than bread, or gave nothing at all—you have an open invitation to be adopted by the perfect Father, and His love is unconditional. As an adopted child of God, you can stand before Him and ask with confidence. It may take some time, and practice, to feel comfortable praying this way, but it's worth the effort to learn how. You'll be following His invitation.

Jesus said, "Ask and it will be given to you; seek and you will find; knock and the door will be opened to you. For everyone who asks receives; he who seeks finds; and to him who knocks, the door will be opened. . . . If you believe, you will receive whatever you ask for in prayer" (Matthew 7:7–8; 21:22).

Does this mean it's ok to pray for a million dollars and expect to receive it? Hardly. Jesus' exhortation in Matthew 21 came just after He cleared the temple of all the money changers and merchants. Jesus wasn't showing us the secret to unleashing material wealth—pray for a Mini Cooper and you'll get one—He instructed us about *what* to pray for in other places in Scripture. I believe His statement had everything to do with *how* we pray. It's about our posture. It's about our faith and believing that if we're following the guidelines He gave us for *what*, we can ask boldly, believing our prayers will be answered.

One woman I met recently had a change of mind that changed the way she prayed. "I prayed and asked God to bring me a husband many times in the past, but I think the Lord changed my perspective to really seek Him for an answer. My mom once said I should pray, 'Lord, have mercy on me.' At first I thought this sounded like I was desperate and demanding God to bring me a husband. But then I realized that was exactly the attitude I needed to have before Him. I *needed* to 'cast my burden on the Lord.' So I began to pray this prayer, and, as I did, I realized that not only did it increase my faith for God's provision, but it also made me excited to see how God would answer. I believe my intimacy with Him increased during this time as I sought to surrender my desires. God changed me as I prayed to Him; my vision of Him began to override my vision of myself. One verse that spoke to me during this time was Psalm 37:5, 'Commit your way to the Lord; trust in him, and he will act' (ESV). What a wonderful promise from Him."

If you're worried you have too little faith, remember the mustard seed. Jesus said, "I tell you the truth, if you have faith as small as a mustard seed, you can say to this mountain, 'Move from here to there' and it will move. Nothing will be impossible for you" (Matthew 17:20). If your faith is smaller even still, ask for more. You can follow the example of the father who wanted Jesus to heal his son. Possessed from his childhood by an evil spirit, he said to Jesus, " 'If you can do anything, take pity on us and help us.' 'If you can'? said Jesus. 'Everything is possible for him who believes.' Immediately the boy's father exclaimed, 'I do believe; help me overcome my unbelief!' " (Mark 9:22–24). After that, Jesus drove the spirit out and healed the boy.

THE LIST OF THIRTY

One friend heard me talking about praying for marriage and decided to take it a step further. I met Sharon at a Bible study where the topics of marriage and motherhood came up often. In the group of thirteen, four of the women were never married. Sharon was one of them.

"I remember in Bible study how you were talking one day about praying boldly," Sharon said. "I was already praying for myself and my single friends. When I thought of it, I prayed for them. But talking to you helped me get serious about things." Sharon listed all her unmarried friends who desired marriage— thirty in all—and on January 1, 2006, she e-mailed everyone on the list. She told them about her plan—a commitment from everyone on the list, to pray for everyone on the list—and asked them to join.

Not everyone was enthusiastic. Some of her friends had to pray about praying before they agreed. To them it was such a bold, untried approached that they worried about putting God on their timetable or demanding something of Him. Others knew He was capable but wondered if He'd do it for them. Still Sharon went forward. "God put the idea on my heart, and I was eager to follow through. James says, 'We do not have because we do not ask,' and I realized I didn't want to be single simply because I wasn't asking God for a husband."

By February she had e-mailed out the official prayer list to the girls and except for one who declined the invitation to join, they were praying.

"Never had I heard of thirty women joining together like this to share their prayers, fears, challenges, and joys as they went on dates, had failed relationships, etc.," Sharon recalls. "But it worked. When we started, only one of the women on the list was dating. One year later, out of thirty women, six were married or engaged to be married, and one was dating." (At press time, one and a half years after they began praying, six of the women are married, five are engaged including Sharon, and five are seriously dating. That's over half the list!)

For all the damage done by two generations of feminist activism, think of the positive change that could come if a generation of women prayed faithfully for godly marriages. When you pray, it changes you, transforming your character and making it possible to live daily like you're planning to marry. But beyond that, such prayer can transform a whole community: families, churches, small groups, college campuses, workplaces, wherever the faithfully praying women spend their time. Imagine in the midst of our postmarriage culture, small countercultures springing up where marriage is honored, men are respectfully motivated, women are cherished, mentors are working on your behalf, purity is esteemed; in short, where everyone is striving for the set-apart life Paul described in 1 Thessalonians 3:11–4:8.

THERE'S BOLD, AND THEN THERE'S BOLD

Isn't it dangerous to pray with such fervor? What if God doesn't answer with a husband after all? Won't it damage the faith of the pray-er? I believe it's worth the risk of disappointment to pray boldly.

In his book *Little Lamb, Who Made Thee?* author and pastor Walter Wangerin Jr. tells the story of a little boy, his godson, who has a growth on his thigh bone. In the midst of waiting for all the medical tests and results, the boy's parents pray intensely, passionately, fervently for healing for their son. Remarkably, someone questions the wisdom of all this prayer.

Wangerin writes, "Someone worried about the intensity of your parents' praying. He said, 'But what if the boy's too sick? What if he doesn't get well? Doesn't it scare you that you might lose your faith if God doesn't answer the prayer?' "

That reminds me of the comments I often hear from singles who wonder if it's OK to pray with insistence, intensity, and passion for a husband. It's like Sharon's friend who wasn't sure it was OK to spend a year praying for a husband for herself and her thirty single friends. She needed to pray about whether it was OK to pray about that. But that's exactly the kind of praying Jesus told us to practice. (Think Bartimaeus and the persistent widow in Luke 18.)

Wangerin goes on:

Your parents said, "We will pray for our son."

You see, Brandon, this was their faith: not that they felt God had to heal you on account of prayer, but rather that they wanted never to stand apart from God, especially not now.

Their prayer was meant neither as a demand nor as magic, neither an ultimatum nor manipulation of the Deity. It was love. It was their highest expression of faith—not faith in your healing, Brandon (though they yearned for that) but faith in God. . . .

Your parents' faith did not depend upon God's "correct" answer to their prayer. Instead, the reality of their prayer depended upon their faith.[2]

REAL MARRIAGE

An old proverb warns, "Be careful what you pray for—you just might get it." In the case of praying for a spouse, I'd say, "Be aware of what you pray for—you might just get it." There's so much misinformation about what marriage is that lots of couples marry with unrealistic or warped expectations. The purpose of marriage isn't companionship, romance, or even sex. Marriage is, in the words of J. Budziszewski, "a divinely blessed and covenantally sealed procreative partnership."[3] And the procreating has everything to do with being refined toward holiness.

With all the confusion about what marriage is for, it's possible that unanswered prayers for spouses have more to do with unrealistic expectations than God's power to supply mates. If you're praying for a spouse thinking he will solve all your problems and meet all your needs, an unanswered prayer may be more of a blessing than you realize. In 1 Corinthians, just after Paul exhorts those who do marry that they haven't sinned, he warns them "those who marry will face many troubles in this life" (7:28).

Asking God to help you find a mate is asking Him to take you from a place of single focus to one that will require selflessness. Far from being the answer to all your dreams and fantasies, marriage will be a crucible for making you more like Christ. But it's not all hard. In the midst of the refining, marriage also provides the opportunity for friendship, companionship, romance, love, fun, and yes, sex.

We know God designed us for relational intimacy—when Adam didn't find a "suitable helper" among the animals, God created Eve. In doing so, He gave us marriage (Genesis 2:24). Marriage is not a social construct. It is a gift from God.

Once you've embraced the calling of marriage, recognized the damage of the fall, remembered God's faithfulness, and accepted His redemption; when you're living like you're planning to marry, being intentional about discipleship, and looking for ways to support those around you—especially men—in their roles, then you can pray boldly. Pray boldly for yourself and for your friends in Christ to esteem marriage, for your community to accept its role in reversing the postmarriage culture, for godly men to grow in their role, for God to do His redemptive work in your life to prepare you to be a godly wife as you trust His ways, and for belief that He *can* help you get married. Some are called to celibate service, and they're specially gifted to live that out. But the rest of us are called to marriage. Asking God for a mate is asking Him for something He created and called very good. For those of us who are called to marriage, it's nothing more than asking Him to give us what He wants us to have.

Steve's story

BY STEVE WATTERS

I think I had a decent education about Christian marriage growing up. My parents were crazy about each other and often embarrassed my brothers and me, acting like teenagers in love. My dad was a pastor who often preached about the principles of Christian marriage. They both encouraged us to be gentlemen in our dating relationships. I attended a Christian college that discouraged sexual activity among its unmarried students, and I likely took a class that talked about Christian marriage (though I honestly can't remember).

Even with all that preparation, somehow my education proved inadequate. By the fall of 1995, I was moving to Virginia to attend Regent University, in the midst of an unraveling marriage engagement. I had always known I wanted to get married someday, but the demise of my engagement reminded me again how little I knew about who would make a good spouse and what my role was in taking a relationship to marriage. It was in that frame of mind that I heard Dr. Morken's encouragement to "get married, make babies, and do government."

I remember appreciating the chutzpah he showed in saying something so countercultural. It sounded like one of those red-meat messages I enjoyed hearing from conservative congressmen and radio talk-show hosts at the time. What made it different was that it was both a public and a personal message. Dr. Morken explained that our corporate decisions about getting married, having kids, and getting involved in public policy would have a ripple effect on generations to come. It wasn't until a few months later that I started to see the personal application.

Dr. Morken's encouragement came from the Genesis command to "be fruitful and multiply," something he presented as "the creation mandate." Marriage as a mandate sounded terribly unromantic, in the same camp as arranged marriages and mail-order brides. Thinking about marriage as a calling, however, caused me to start rethinking my attitude and actions toward marriage. But it's not the only thing that was a challenge to my beliefs. So was Candice.

Candice caught my eye early on, but not for the reason she would have wanted. She was introduced at student orientation as some kind of job networking assistant who had come to Regent after working on Capitol Hill. I remember thinking she was cute, but the more dominant impression I got was that she was some kind of power woman. I think it had something to do with her businesslike demeanor, her short metro-looking haircut and the shoulder pads in her jacket. Of course, it could also have been that I was jealous of her real-world political experience and the fact that she had landed an important-sounding role, even though she was as new to the program as I was. When Candice started sharing her strong opinions in the classes we had together, I remember thinking, *She's a fireball.* I had been raised a polite southerner and wasn't surprised to find out that she grew up north of the Mason-Dixon Line.

Our first promising conversation came a few weeks later when we started talking in the middle of a boring library tour. It was one of the first clicks I remember experiencing with another graduate student. Turned out we both enjoyed reading, and we chatted about a Douglas Coupland book I was working through at the time. A little later I went out to eat with a group of classmates. Candice sat down beside me. In the course of conversation, I found out some other things we had in common—we had both been yearbook editors and we were born one day apart in the same year.

What really boosted my connection with Candice was the time we spent working together, along with four other classmates, to launch an online magazine. In this setting, we found a kinship in our shared interest in cultural trends, new media, and entrepreneurial ventures. One of the highlights of that launching season was an excursion we took with our team to Williamsburg, Virginia. It was a crisp fall day and the massive gnarled trees between the colonial buildings and gardens were filled with blazing leaves. We couldn't resist climbing up into one of them and spreading out over the limbs for a team photo. Sipping hot cider, we strolled through the historical grounds getting to know each other and dreaming up our new venture.

Riding together on the hour-long drive to and from Williamsburg, I had no trouble coming up with conversation with Candice. In fact, it felt like spending time with a childhood friend. I guess that's why I didn't think it was out of the ordinary to tell her that I had a date that night with one of her friends.

Despite our close connection, Candice wasn't registering in the part of my brain that triggered infatuation. Even in my mid-twenties I couldn't explain why I was so often attracted to women who were fun to go out with but proved to be a bad fit for marriage. Like the girl I dated in college who would throw rocks at my dorm room window as a greeting (it was a Christian college thing) and then run off with the guy who lived in the room below me if I wasn't home. This irrational part of me generated doubletakes and obsessive thoughts about women who fit into my version of the "ideal woman template." Some of my template came from expectations I developed while growing up (such as favoring the long brown hair, southern hospitality, and nurturing spirit of my mom); but I suspect a lot of it came from my cultural "education" that held up physical perfection and flirtatious personalities.

Even though I wasn't registering any romantic sparks, Candice and I continued getting to know each other through our classes and Webzine work. In those settings we felt a certain familiarity and collegiality growing around the shared worldview and sense of mission we were developing. But then something changed.

The fact that we'd both been college yearbook editors had been a strong point of connection for us, until Candice edited me. Instead of penciling in a few improvements on an article I wrote for the Webzine, it looked like she had slashed and burned the thing. I didn't even recognize my article anymore. This annoyed me and created some tension between us for a while.

I stopped seeing her around as much. She was spending a lot of time with another guy. I'd see them on campus having long, intense-looking conversations. I thought maybe they were starting to date. She called one afternoon during that period and asked if we could get together. We went down to a restaurant on Virginia Beach to talk. Turns out, the guy she'd been spending all that time with didn't want to take their friendship any further. She said something that night I found rather bold: "I'm going to be a good wife for some guy. Why couldn't he see it?"

We didn't see the irony at the time, but Candice started shifting her attention from one guy friend to another, and we started hanging out again. In fact, we got to the point where we were spending nearly all our free time together. We went to movies, to the beach, out to eat, to jazz festivals, and to numerous coffee bars.

What was crazy to me is that our time together deepened our connection but also revealed differences I wasn't sure what to do with. We could see how much our attitudes had been shaped by the fact that Candice was the oldest of five and I was the youngest of three (although I was born only a few minutes after my twin, and my older brother was only fifteen months ahead of us). Also as the daughter of a dentist, Candice had gotten used to a higher-end lifestyle than I did as the son of a small-town pastor.

Temperamentally, Candice was a goal-focused leader with strong opinions, while I was an even-keeled, easygoing bridge builder. I had a hard time knowing what to do with her bold opinions—especially about popular culture. Back then the show *Seinfeld* was still on prime time. In the same way some guys have a *Godfather* line for everything, I frequently made *Seinfeld* references. One night Candice questioned my *Seinfeld* indulgence—as well as some popular movies I had mentioned enjoying. She observed that my media diet didn't seem consistent with my faith and speculated that TV was having a bad influence on my ideas about relationships.

Even with so many differences in view, something kept drawing me back to Candice. While she didn't appear to fit my "ideal woman template," I kept finding myself forming a deeper connection with her. I didn't realize at the time how much it had to do with Candice, but I was getting back on my feet again. After showing up for grad school discouraged and listless from a broken engagement, I was starting to feel new life. I was dreaming again about the future.

I can't remember how long this stage of our relationship went on—of spending time with Candice and enjoying a fresh, hopeful perspective on life—but I was enjoying it. Until Candice brought it to an abrupt end. That's the point at which she asked me to clarify what our time together meant. She said she wanted to get married and couldn't just stay in a perpetual buddy relationship. "I need you to call this what it is," she said. "Are we dating or not?"

Well, I didn't know exactly. If she had been one of the girls who had set my infatuation alarm off, I probably would have said, "Yes, we are dating." But this was different. Our relationship hadn't started off that way. I wasn't infatuated; I was just becoming increasingly attracted and connected while I tried to figure out what to do with all the differences between us.

I asked her for some time to pray about it, and we planned to reconnect that night.

I hoped as I prayed that God would give me a clear sign about what I should do. Growing up, I heard my parents tell their story of God intervening miraculously to bring them together. My dad was in a rock band at the time, but he still had enough Christian faith in him that he often sensed God directing him. One day, he told his family that he felt a strong leading to go to a particular church in town because God was going to show him his future wife there. His family went to the church, and after the service my dad introduced himself to the piano player. Then he asked her out. She already had another date, but my dad talked her into breaking it. He proposed only a couple of weeks later. His confidence in God's leading kept him from having any doubts.

I didn't get an audible word or obvious sign from God that day, but I did get something else. First, I felt a sense of embarrassment. I realized I hadn't been a gentleman in how I had treated Candice. I began to see the confusion I had caused her as I enjoyed our time together, while keeping my options open for other opportunities. My posture toward Candice had told other guys that she wasn't available to them, even though I wasn't being a good steward of the availability she was giving me. The other thing I sensed as I prayed was that we had more potential than I realized. Even though I hadn't figured out what to do about all our differences, I felt new appreciation for what drew us together. The roots of our friendship had grown deeply, and we had something I didn't want to lose.

What I did have to lose was my casual, low-risk approach. I needed to be all in. I had to start giving our potential all my attention. Instead of just hanging out, I had to be more intentional about what we were doing together. I told Candice that night that I wanted us to make it official, to call our relationship what it was, and find out if we had the potential for a good marriage.

That wasn't the end of our challenges, but it was the end of the first chapter of our relationship—the one you could call "the pseudo-relationship, buddy period." It helped us move into a time when we could gauge what we had. Instead of letting our differences keep me on the sidelines, I grew more able to face them directly—to see if they were deal breakers or possibly something that could be a source of strength.

In this process, things changed with my "ideal woman template." In some areas, Candice changed. She didn't know how much I liked long brown hair. I didn't realize that she decided to let her hair grow when she started at Regent, and I was growing more attracted to her as it did. I also watched her power persona soften somewhat. She was still bold and confident, but she let me see a soft, nurturing side I hadn't noticed before. In other areas, I changed. I became more aware of the irrational impulses that had been driving my infatuations and recognized how they often lured me toward style over substance. In place of those impulses, I learned to appreciate the scope of Candice's substance, even while I started to value her distinct style. Spending the most time I ever had with someone from outside the South helped me get over my bias for southern girls. I also began to appreciate how our differences in personality and birth order (and even editing styles) weren't threats as much as healthy balances to each other.

The last hurdle I had to clear centered in my concern that Candice was a stronger leader than I was. I worried that she was so much more driven than me and that I would have a hard time stepping into the leadership role Christian men are called to take in marriage. Looking back, I can't remember if Candice started making adjustments in how she related to me or if I just started seeing things differently. Somehow, though, I began to interpret her drive in our relationship not as a threat but as motivation for me to be the best I could be. I learned to appreciate how she had the ability to push me in a positive way and encourage me to be a leader. Even in challenges like our confrontation over *Seinfeld* and other pop culture, I valued that she believed I could do better. In areas like my career, where I had been intimidated by her earlier expectation of marrying a doctor, I felt emboldened to discover the potential she saw in me. More and more, I wanted to be the man she believed I was capable of becoming. I wanted to believe that we had the stuff of a good marriage—that our deep friendship could grow into a love affair. Even though I never had the kind of "burning bush" my dad had, I felt the peace that God was weaving our lives together— including all our differences.

Most important, I came to see what Candice had seen much earlier—that the passions and callings we had shared all along could best be channeled through marriage.

In February 1997, I took Candice back to Williamsburg. In the middle of one of the enchanting colonial gardens, I got down on one knee and repeated my favorite line from *When Harry Met Sally*: "When you've met the person you want to spend the rest of your life with, you want the rest of your life to start as soon as possible."

Just the week before, I gave Candice a poem I wrote for her called "Love Feast." In it I tried to describe what had happened over the last year and a half of our relationship—how she had faithfully believed in our potential for marriage even though my appetite for a deep, meaningful connection had been spoiled by the "fast food" of cultural expectations, keeping me from enjoying the truly gourmet.

I used to feast on simple fare
Tame, light spice . . . just heavy garnish.
Often I'd add a cup of sugar
But it seldom covered the bitter aftertaste.
It was hard to break old patterns,
Harder still to try new things.
But you were persistent and confident
Baby steps, baby bites, and sips.
"Try this," you offered often—
A great chef with the patience of Job.
"Too hot," I'd say; "too spicy" I'd add
As I kept one eye open for a fast and easy meal.
But then the old became bland
While you served up freshness—alive with flavor.
Sweet but not sticky, bold but not bitter.
Fulfilling my appetite, you restored my strength.
Now the appetizers have led to the feast,
Where you've prepared an overflowing table before me
Flavors I never expected—aromas that overwhelm.
And I long to sit at your table all the days of my life.

I can't thank Candice enough for believing in us enough to persist, and for making possible the past ten years of life we've shared at our table.

Applying *Get Married* to Your Story: Commonly Asked Questions

Establishing Relationships

Q: Is there *one* predestined spouse for you or do you just get to choose from the possibilities that come your way?

I don't know if there's only one for each of us. In theory it seems we could make a good life with a variety of husbands—if we're willing to do the work necessary for any good relationship. The only requirement Scripture gives for a marriage partner is that we be equally yoked. Beyond that, it's mostly common sense and hard work. Choosing a mate is about making the most of the opportunities you encounter—or in the manner of olden days, choosing the most eligible man in your village.

It's tempting to think there's one perfect man—a "soul mate"—for each of us. It's certainly a romantic ideal, but not very practical. And this ideal carries a host of dangers; the most obvious being that if you think you've found "the one," how do you explain the difficult times that arise—and they will—after you say "I do"? Even perfectly matched couples will encounter trials in their relationship. The Bible promises as much. (First Corinthians 7:28 says, "But if you do marry, you have not sinned; and if a virgin marries, she has not sinned. But those who marry will face many troubles in this life, and I want to spare you this.")

For this reason, you should look for the confirmation of friends and family that the man you've chosen is a good match. And you should be better as a couple than you are apart: emotionally, mentally, and spiritually. Finally, since Scripture commands wives to respect their husbands, you should choose a man you admire and are able to respect, even when he doesn't deserve it. (See Ephesians 5:22–33 for more on this.)

The answer to the question, *Is there just one?* remains a mystery. But you can know for certain that once you are married, whomever you've wed *becomes* the one. At that point you are committed for life.

Q: Should I wait until a guy makes it crystal clear that he is interested, or should I give signals that I am interested so that he may continue to move forward?

It's unlikely that you're not giving him any signals at all. When your heart starts leaning toward a man, it's virtually impossible not to give signals that you like him.

Q: While I feel that guys should make the first moves in wooing a girl, I find myself having to hint to the guy that I like him. How do I know if he feels the same way about me?

If you have to ask, he probably doesn't. Guys, like girls, tend to show their affection naturally. Even if he hasn't asked you out yet, if he pays more attention to you than other girls in the room, sits next to you when the opportunity arises, or asks you to sit next to him, and asks you questions that draw you out and seems genuinely interested in your answers, he probably likes you. If you respond in kind, and he's secure, he'll likely initiate a

get married

more formal relationship. Just be patient. It's his job to lead, and if you jump the gun, assuming this role, you'll be establishing an unsettling pattern.

Q: How should a woman let a man know she's interested without being too aggressive? I do believe that men need to take the lead in relationships, but these days most men don't seem to want to take the risk unless they are "guaranteed" success. Do my signals need to be stronger?

You're right that men want to know you won't let them fall flat on their face. But ultimately, the risk required to initiate a relationship *is* the man's to take. By all means, be kind. Be approachable. Ask him questions about himself: what he likes and what he hopes to become. You're probably already doing all this; more or stronger wouldn't necessarily be better. (And sparing him the possibility of failure won't boost his manhood; it may undermine it.) Unless you are painfully shy, chances are he knows you're interested. Now it's up to him to act on that knowledge.

Q: There's a guy who everyone says is right for me. I totally agree, except we aren't dating officially. We hang out together and have a great time. People think we're dating, but I know we're not. What can I do to let him know that I'm interested in a relationship? I've always thought that it's the guy who's supposed to do the asking, but I'm not sure.

I can say with confidence that the best way to motivate your male friend to "make things official" is to back off from spending so much time with him. If everyone thinks you're dating, then you're probably acting like you are. But by giving him so much access to your time, affection, and intimate friendship—without requiring any commitment on his part—you're removing all the incentives for him to be forthright about his intentions.

You're right, it is the guy who's supposed to do the asking—don't violate your instincts on this one. By giving him less attention you may actually create the circumstances that will embolden him to act honorably toward you.

And if he doesn't, you've saved yourself from any more wasted time with a guy whose behavior indicates he's not interested in moving your friendship toward marriage.

Q: Proverbs says "A man who *finds* a wife finds a good thing." Why does it seem like most Christian men aren't looking for Christian wives?

There's the problem of our culture that glorifies extended adolescence and the "freedom" of being single. Examples that model healthy, rewarding, godly marriage are harder to find. Then there's the lack of encouragement and expectations from friends, parents, and even the church to marry well. Most guys simply haven't been told that marriage is something they should pursue. Finally (keep in mind this is the simplified list), most women in a guy's universe are content to date recreationally and remain "just friends" indefinitely.

It's not that men have changed—they've always needed incentives to commit to one woman for life—but the standards have been lowered. Until the women in a community (church, university, office, peer group, etc.) band together to raise a new standard of "no intimacy, friendship, or otherwise, without the commitment of serious dating toward marriage," guys will settle for getting their needs met outside of marriage.

The good news is that as single women, there are things you and your friends can do—actions you can take—that may improve your lot. Stop settling for friendships that feel like dating relationships but aren't. Stop giving away pieces of your heart without being asked. Stop being intimate—physically or emotionally—with men who are not your husband. Start insisting that to gain intimacy, men must act honorably, state their intentions, and initiate official relationships with the goal being marriage.

Q: The guys in my church aren't marriage material, and bars are out, so where can a marriage-minded woman go to meet eligible men?

You say the men in your church aren't marriage material. While it's possible there aren't any strong candidates for marriage among those in your congregation, your description of the men makes me wonder about your expectations. What characteristics do you consider worthwhile? What makes for good husband material? It's important to weigh your answers against the standards of Scripture. What does God consider "husband material"? Traits like integrity, honesty, and maturity come to mind; also willingness to leave father and mother in order to form a new family; ability to work hard and provide for a wife and children; openness to babies; and willingness to sacrifice for wife and children—the very thing Christ modeled in His sacrifice for our sin.

Is your church an environment that encourages and celebrates marriage? If so, even a lack of single men may not be reason enough to leave it. What about the older members? They may have sons, nephews, grandsons, etc., they could introduce you to. In the end, it's not so much "where you go" to find a mate, but who you know and what they know about you. (For more about this, see chapter 4, "You Need a Network".)

The most important thing you can do is pray. I've talked about this at length in chapter 8, "Pray Boldly". While you're at it, consider praying about a change of locale. I did. When I was twenty-five I moved from my small hometown to a larger city where I attended a Christian graduate school. I was hoping to meet someone of like heart and mind. Thankfully, I did. Being in a new place afforded lots of opportunities to meet new people. And to meet men while pursuing something I loved helped increase the odds that I'd have a lot in common with them.

Whether it's pursuing an advanced degree or developing a hobby, focus on activities you enjoy. You're more likely to find someone with similar interests if you're engaged in an activity you both enjoy when you meet.

If you're a true homebody and settling in a new city or even planning a night on the town sounds dreadful, host some events in your home. Consider inviting a few single guys and girls over for a dinner party or a game night or to help you paint your living room a new color. The added bonus is that by playing hostess, you'll get to display some of your unique talents in a very obvious and complimentary way. It's a lot harder to let a guy know you're a great chef if you always meet at restaurants. Challenge everyone to bring one friend who will be new to the group. That way everyone has the chance to meet someone new.

Q: What about meeting guys online?

It's hard to resist Internet matching services that claim they'll help you find: "your soul mate," "the perfect love you were born to meet," "satisfying marriage," and more. And sometimes they do. If you're going to use an online service, it's best to limit yourself to sites that have marriage as their goal. Just remember what these sites are good at—quickly providing a lot of potential introductions to eligible believers who are also interested in marriage; and what they're not good at—discerning the character of all those potential matches, protecting your heart from premature intimacy, solving the problem of long distance, and revealing a candidate's flaws as well as all his self-selected pluses.

If you're having trouble meeting eligible men where you live,

get married

and decide to give an online service a try, remember these basics:

Use a Christian site. You don't have to sacrifice quality of service—some Christian sites are among the best services available—and you're more likely to find a match with whom you can be "equally yoked."

Trust, but verify. A long online profile is a fine place to start getting to know someone's character, but the best sources are their friends and family. Get the input of the people who know your match well.

Don't rush it. Some counselors recommend spending at least a year living in the same city as someone you've met online. It takes time to get to know someone—in their environment—well enough to know if they're capable of a lifelong commitment.

God designed us for marriage. The ultimate creative Spirit, He's not limited in how He does it. Sometimes He works through a matchmaking service, sometimes He uses a relative or friend to play matchmaker. Though you won't find any Bible verses about online dating, you will find principles for conducting relationships in a way that honors Him. Seek to honor God in your pursuit of marriage, and He'll direct your steps.

Q: How much of an age difference is too much for a guy who's younger than me? What about one who's older?

That depends on how old you are. Although a five-year difference either direction may be imperceptible when you're thirty-five, when you're twenty-three a man five years your junior would not only be noticeable, but legally problematic. Also, given that women tend to mature faster than men (this is, of course, a general trend, not a hard-and-fast rule), it's not probable that at age twenty-three you'd find an equitable level of maturity in a man so much younger than you. Conversely, your ability to relate and effectively partner with a man older than you will be more likely the older you are. I think for most women, when they're in their early twenties, they should date someone close in age; no more than a few years difference. As you get older, assuming both you and he are spiritually mature, the difference becomes less of an issue.

As women age, the potential for good matches with men who are younger increases. I have quite a few friends who've married men five years or more their junior, and they have good marriages. Once you're past college, it's not so much a matter of years but of maturity and compatibility. A lot of life experience tends to happen between eighteen and twenty-three—the kinds of things that have the ability to grow a person up, if you let them. Also, if you are older, that doesn't mean the role of leader in the relationship should shift to you. The man should always be the initiator. Then it's up to you to decide how you will respond. Especially if you're older, allowing the man to lead is paramount to the success of any romantic relationship.

Q: Is it wise to date someone who has less formal education than I do?

This question isn't surprising considering more women than men are attending college these days.[1] I think it's critical to make the distinction between a man who is uneducated and one who didn't graduate from college or acquire as many degrees as you have.

There are many ways to get an education, college being but one of them. And the formality of going to college is no guarantee that someone is truly educated. Many schools today do little more than prepare their students for the workplace (and some employers argue they're not even doing that well). There's a lot more to developing your mind and intellect than learning how to make money for an employer.

I think the better question has to do with your intellectual compatibility. Are the two of you on the same, or similar, intellectual

get married

plane? Are you able to communicate at the same level about topics of shared interest? Is he intelligent and committed to the Lord? That may be worth a lot more than "graduated from college."

Two other things to consider: Why did he forgo or quit college, and how does he feel about your education? If he decided to teach himself by reading great books and spent the four years that some young men waste on frat parties building a business, I'd say that's worth more than college. But if a man didn't go because he couldn't get in, or thought it would be too hard, or was tired of reading challenging books and learning, I'd say that's a major red flag.

The second consideration is his attitude toward your degree. Does he affirm you in your learning and take pride in what you've achieved? Does he encourage you to keep growing in your knowledge and understanding? Or is he threatened by the fact that you've accomplished something he hasn't? Does he avoid the subject of education or act agitated if it comes up? Again, those are red flags.

In the end, I think, *Did he go to college?* is the wrong question. The better question is, *Do you respect him and, ultimately, see yourself submitting to him?*

This is not to say Christian women have to submit to all men, of course. After they leave the covering of their father, the Bible only requires that they submit to one man: their husband.[2] So choose wisely. It's not likely you'll want to follow the lead of a man who is inferior in the realm of thinking, reasoning, and decision making. College degrees notwithstanding, it's essential that you marry a man you respect. Common sense says marry a man who is at least equal to you intellectually.

Q: What if a guy is interested in me, but I can tell he's financially irresponsible?

In addition to "getting to know someone," an important part of dating is observing a man's character. Just as he should be assessing your interest in being a life giver to his potential children, you should be weighing his ability to provide.

Some men will provide a blue-collar living and others a more professional salary. There's no magic number that admits men to the "able to marry category." But any man interested in marrying needs to be able to provide the basics for living not only for himself, but for a wife and future children.

A man's ability to either make the budget sacrifices necessary to pay for your coffees, movie tickets, and sandwiches—or to be creative in stretching his resources to pull off a special event with a couple of bucks—is an important cue for the future. If he says he likes you but can't afford to date you, you have to wonder what would change so he could afford to marry you. If marriage is "too expensive," and the whole goal of dating is to find a mate, why waste time dating him?

That's not to say every date has to consist of dinner at a five-star restaurant and a Broadway show, but it is a man's responsibility to provide. If he's unable to do so for once- or twice-a-week outings, it begs the question: What will he be like as a husband?

A man who is pursuing a woman for dates should already be convinced of his readiness to marry in a timely manner. And that includes the ability to pay for the outings.

In our culture, we often think it's sexist to expect men to be providers—since women are obviously able to make substantial financial contributions of their own. However, even though women are capable of providing, it's men who bear the ultimate responsibility to do so within a family. In fact, 1 Timothy 5:8 says that a man who doesn't provide for his family is worse than an unbeliever.

Q: Are long-distance relationships wise?

Given the mobility of the twentysomething years, beginning with college and proceeding through early career developments, it's not uncommon to face seasons of separation from romantic interests and long-distance love.

Though maintaining a healthy relationship has added challenges, there are some benefits to being in different cities, at least for a short season.

One of the best things about distance is that it can go a long way toward keeping you pure. It can also make the longings stronger, though, so you have to be extra vigilant to set up good boundaries when you are together (like being together in public and in groups).

For postcollege readers who are in long-distance relationships because their jobs are keeping them in different cities, I'd add a caution. Long-term, long-distance can artificially delay progress. If you're apart for long months or years, you may remain "a couple" without ever moving toward marriage. To do so in your twenties is to potentially waste your most marriageable years. Anything past a year is a no-win. In the event you do eventually marry, you may have squandered your fertility during the waiting. If you eventually break up, you may have missed out on other good offers of marriage.

Q: I know preoccupation with looks is a problem, but is it possible to think about beauty too little?

Yes. There are lots of Christian women who struggle with the problem of overemphasis on beauty. And the consequences that follow are ugly. (See Ezekiel 16 and Isaiah 3:16–26.) But others fall into the category of mismanagement or neglect. And this may have a profound effect on a woman's desire for marriage and family.

Men are visual. More than most women, most men are stimulated, animated, and activated by what they *see*. It's hard for women to fully grasp what this means because it's not our nature to be equally aroused by the images around us. We're more relational. Some people insist there is no difference between men and women. And our hypersexualized culture has altered the way some, even many, women react to what their eyes see. But generally speaking, men get their primary input through their eyes, while we get it through our hearts and minds.

This is not to say it's OK for men to be sexually aroused by any and all women. Jesus was clear that lust is a sin, saying, "everyone who looks at a woman with lust for her has already committed adultery with her in his heart" (Matthew 5:28 NASB). But it follows that Jesus knew He needed to address the issue of looking at a woman with lust because He knows of a man's propensity for it.

Still, knowing that men have to fight their sin nature (Job 31:1) is not justification for women to neglect their outward appearance. Being overweight and unkempt does little to attract a man's attention and ultimately, affection. There are men for whom externals mean nothing. But most men do want to marry a woman they find attractive. And it's not just that they want someone pleasant to look at. How you care for your externals sends powerful messages to men about your stewardship of what God's given you.

This is not, however, about the world's standard of beauty. It's about making the most of your natural assets. Men are as varied in their taste as women are. Some like a more natural, clean-scrubbed look while others appreciate the enhancements of makeup. Some go for athletic and lean, others prefer a rounder, more huggable woman. You should not fear that if you embrace whatever loveliness God has given you, you will fail to appeal to a man.

The kind of man a godly woman should want to marry would esteem a woman who strives to be lovely, both inside and out.

Choosing a Mate

Q: How should I pursue a godly marriage if I have already "gone all the way"?

By creating circumstances that ensure purity from now on. (Incidentally, the following advice goes for everyone in dating relationships, whether virgins or not.)

The most practical way comes straight from Scripture. First Thessalonians 5:6–8, 22–24 says,

So then, let us not be like others, who are asleep, but let us be alert and self-controlled. For those who sleep, sleep at night, and those who get drunk, get drunk at night. But since we belong to the day, let us be self-controlled, putting on faith and love as a breastplate, and the hope of salvation as a helmet.

Avoid every kind of evil. May God himself, the God of peace, sanctify you through and through. May your whole spirit, soul and body be kept blameless at the coming of our Lord Jesus Christ. The one who calls you is faithful and he will do it (italics added).

In the KJV that italicized line reads, "Abstain from all appearance of evil." In addition to the many prohibitions against actual sexual immorality, this passage stands out because it tells us to stay away from even the appearance of it. I believe that's because to avoid even what seems evil has the benefit of guarding your reputation. No one will suspect you've been fooling around if you conduct yourselves honorably, where all can see. If you're never behind closed doors, you're not giving anyone the opportunity to wonder what you're up to.

But also, I believe God commanded this because He knows that often the "appearance of evil"—even in the absence of actual sin—occurs in the context of circumstances where sin is more likely, or at least very accessible. If you or he has a habit of sleeping over, even if it's on the couch, people will start to assume you're doing more than sleeping. Nothing may be going on, but it looks like something is. That's "the appearance of evil," and Scripture says to avoid it.

It's tempting at this point to shift the focus to all those gossips who should just mind their own business. But the Bible doesn't give us that option. And for good reason. When you're really honest, you have to admit that situations that most obviously lend themselves to speculation are the very setups most likely to lead to sin.

It really is tough, as you've discovered, to turn off the sex drive. In fact, that's the way God designed it. Hand holding is supposed to lead to hugging is supposed to lead to kissing is supposed to lead to fondling and, well, you get the idea. And within marriage, this progression isn't a problem. But when you're just dating, the momentum leads to all sorts of trouble.

So what should you do about it? Avoid it, just like Scripture advises; avoid the opportunity to get carried away. And the only way I know to do that is to not be alone together. It sounds so old-fashioned. But it really is practical. Spend time together in public places. Go on walks in beautiful parks and around the city center; take in a movie and have lunch at a restaurant, and spend as much time together with each other's families and church families and close friends and mentors as you can. If he's the one, once you're married you'll have the rest of your lives to be alone together behind closed doors with slow music and lots of candlelight.

Rules about lines and limits are important. So is accountability. But the longest list of don'ts won't do you much good if you're always in your apartment at night, just the two of you.

All these practical steps should follow on the heels of seeking God's and your boyfriend's forgiveness for your past sexual sins. Then you can start fresh (Lamentations 3:22–24), with daily prayers for grace and strength to resist temptation (1 Corinthians 10:12–13), including the important decisions about how and where you spend time together.

You've got to set the circumstances for success. And circumstances that appear wholesome and godly usually are.

Q: I just discovered my boyfriend struggles with porn. Is it true that all guys struggle with porn, and therefore, we should just accept it?

In another day pornography was a lot more difficult to obtain. You had to actually ask for it from behind the convenience store counter, or make a drive to some disreputable bookstore in the seedy part of town. For a lot of men, that was more trouble than it was worth. Often the risk to reputation was enough to quiet the temptation.

Today, thanks to the Internet and its lawless environment, porn is ubiquitous. Dr. Albert Mohler, president of the Southern Baptist Theological Seminary, says he just assumes every man entering the seminary has used Internet porn to some extent and addresses it accordingly.

Realistically, I think women need to approach the men in their lives similarly. This is not license to ask just any man about his Internet habits, or to bring up racy topics in mixed company; but it is reason to, at a minimum, ask the man you're seriously dating how he avoids the temptations so prevalent in our society.

Not every man struggles in the same way, or to the same degree. All men face temptation, though, and some are better than others at obeying God's Word about fleeing (see Matthew 26:41 and Job 31:1). Proverbs 28:13 says, "He who conceals his sins does not prosper, but whoever confesses and renounces them finds mercy." What you should be looking for is a man who, if he has struggled with porn, has put it in his past and through confession and turning away, has found mercy. By no means should women just accept that because porn is so widespread, men can't be helped for using it.

Q: How important is it for my parents to give their blessing on a potential spouse?

Ephesians 6:1–3 and Colossians 3:20 tell children to obey their parents "in the Lord, for this is right" and "in all things, for this is well pleasing to the Lord" (NKJV). These go hand in hand with commandment five in Exodus 20:12, "Honor your father and your mother, that your days may be prolonged in the land which the Lord your God gives you" (NASB).

I believe scripturally, the starting point is your (and your boyfriend's) attitude toward your parents. You must continue this conversation and make your decision from a position of honor and respect. They are due that, at a minimum, even if you don't think they deserve it and regardless of what you decide. If you have any doubts about your attitude toward your mom and dad, ask your pastor or mature Christian mentors what they think about your attitude. Is it godly?

Second, your independence: Are you still living at home? Do they contribute financially to you at all? If they are still in a position of provision, you are still under their authority and have an obligation to obey.

Do your parents have legitimate concerns about your maturity or other issues that you need to be working to resolve? Is there any chance you're missing something they see that makes it wiser to wait? If you honestly don't see anything that should prevent you from marrying this man at this time, ask your pastor or mentors if you're missing something. Consider meeting with your parents, along with your mentors, to discuss their reservations. Are there hurdles they want you to clear to prove you're ready to marry? If so, find out what they are and start working to clear them. Hopefully, if this is their rationale, addressing their concerns will allay them.

Practically, it makes a lot of sense to honor and obey your parents. They are, after all, your parents. They will be part of your life for as long as you and they are alive. They will also be the grandparents of your children. These are not roles to discard lightly. If it's simply a matter of timing (e.g., you're still in college or not yet out of their home), rather than character, take heart. Jacob worked seven years before marrying Rachel. The worst-case scenario may be that you wait. If marriage is meant to be, it will still make sense in the future, and the rest of your life together is a long time.

If, however, after getting wise counsel from older, more mature believers (see Titus 2) you are convinced your parents' reasons for asking you to wait are nothing more than personal preference, then you do have the option to proceed without their blessing. Although Scripture defers to parents and requires you give them respect, it doesn't say you must never make a decision contrary to their advice. Once you're eighteen (depending on the state where you marry) you are of the age that you can legally decide to marry against their wishes. But keep in mind the long–term implications of such a decision. Your relationship with them is lifelong and important to the health of your marriage.

Though it would be tragic to marry without their blessing, if they are being truly unbiblical—as testified to by two or more witnesses (Matthew 18:15–17)—it may, in the end, be your only option. It's certainly not ideal, but is at least consistent with the principle of leaving and cleaving (Matthew 19:4–6).

If you decide to proceed with your plans to marry, do so prayerfully and fully aware of what you're walking away from. As much as possible you want to enter marriage with no regrets. Regardless of what you decide, be above reproach in how you relate to your parents. Remember, even if they wrongly prevent your marrying as soon as you'd like, God sees. He will reward your faithfulness.

Pore over the Scriptures for wisdom, keep seeking the counsel of godly mentors, and above all, pray. God can change hearts and minds (yours and your parents) when human efforts at persuasion fail.

Q: Is it wise to delay marriage until you're financially stable?

That depends on what you mean by *stable*. It's understandable, and admirable, that newlyweds want to have a steady income. Being able to pay for heat, electricity, and food is essential.

Sadly, too many singles put off marriage for an elusive goal of financial stability: something most people pursue their whole lives. Financial responsibility is a part of pleasing God, but not at the expense of all His other commands.

In addition to being good stewards, He tells us to marry. He tells young men to pursue marriage (Proverbs 18:22) and couples to be "fruitful and multiply" (Genesis 9:7 NASB); He calls children a "reward" (Psalm 127:3). Even if those things never add to your balance sheet, they enrich your life in ways that dollars never will.

Two can live more economically than one. A newly married couple paying for one apartment can make their money go further than two singles, both working, renting two. Besides, it's a lot more fun to spend your "hungry years" with your best friend and lover.

Life Planning

Q: When I finish school next year, I'll be in the hole at least $50,000. Trouble is, now I want to get married and start a family. What should I do?

Don't panic. Maybe God is filling you with the desire to marry and have children now to motivate you to focus your passion on paying down your debt.

Don't worry. What you owe in student loans is not a surprise to God. He knows what you owe and what you long for. He can help you get there (Matthew 6:25–26).

Don't delay. There's no time to waste in starting to tackle this debt. Marriage may still be a few years off. But if you start on an aggressive plan to pay your loans off now, you'll be in a much better position to marry later.

There are some great Christian financial tools out there that can teach you how to pay off these loans as quickly as possible. Steve and I are working through one of Dave Ramsey's books in an effort to pay off our graduate school loans.

You might also consider taking one of the Crown Financial Ministries' classes offered through many churches. This provides a group setting and the benefit of wise counsel and accountability that a book alone doesn't.

Whatever you do, don't ignore the debt. The sooner you start paying it down, the sooner it will go away. You don't have to be 100 percent debt free to get married (few people are today). I believe the most important question your future husband will ask has to do with your attitude about debt. You need to be more than remorseful. You need to be resourceful. You need to be demonstrating that you are doing all you can to actively pay it off. If he's a good man and sees you behaving responsibly and diligently toward this debt, he will respect you.

Q: I'm twenty-eight and still single, though I'd like to be married. Usually I'm content to focus on my job and furthering my education, but then I'll start wondering what God has in store for me. What's the best way to wait patiently for God's timing for a husband?

Based on all I've read and written, I'm convinced that at this stage, learning patience should not be your goal. If marriage is your goal, it's essential to focus on it at least as much as you do your job and ongoing education.

You say that you wonder about God's will for you in dating and marriage. If you don't have the traits Jesus set forth in Matthew 19 that qualify and equip a believer for lifelong celibacy, then you can be confident His will for you is the same as it is for most believers: get married and have children. I think too often we squander the decade of our twenties wondering *if* it's God's will for us to marry. The irony is that for the vast majority of us, He's already told us quite plainly that it is (Genesis 2; 1 Corinthians 7).

It's time we stop wasting our most marriageable years wondering *if* we're meant for marriage and start doing what we can to get there. I'm not suggesting you find a guy and pop the question. And I'm not unaware that in this fallen world, some women will remain single because of poor decisions on their part or the part of men who might have been their mates. But I am encouraging young women to do what they can. For something as important as marriage, it seems to me we ought to pour at least as much initiative and creativity into the process as we do our college degrees and careers.

Q: I'm studying to become a college professor. If I get married and have children someday, I'd also like to stay home with my children. Am I wasting my time on this degree?

Far better to count the cost of a demanding tenure track before you marry and have children than after. Many women have started down the grueling (yet rewarding) path of becoming a professor only to find their plans derailed when they wanted time off to have babies.

The best advice I can give is to find a woman who is now where you want to be and ask her what it's like. How did she get there? What, if any, sacrifices did she make to achieve her goals? What did she do right? What would she do differently? It will be most beneficial if she is a believer and willing to mentor you along your own journey.

Also, consider that we've been acculturated to believe all of our education, adventure, and fun must be front-loaded if it's to happen at all. The assumption, especially among guys, is that if there's something you really want to do, you'd better get it in before you get married because once you say "I do," the high life is over.

In another day, marriage and family was the adventure. Granted, travel was more limited, as was disposable income. But even today, it's possible to see marriage as the starting point. What could make your goals and mountaintop experiences richer than getting there with your life partner and best friend?

The thing we women mistakenly believe is that life will always be in the future as it is today. But life is long and full of variations. You may have time to complete one or more advanced degrees before you marry (your education will never be wasted on your own children), or you may not. But I don't think settling for an easier major is the solution. If you're blessed with a strong mind and a desire to research, the better approach may well be a willingness to punctuate your education and career advancement with life. If you marry after college and have a few babies, you'll still have plenty of time when they're grown to go back to school. You can pick up where you left off.

Back when I was pregnant with our first child, I couldn't imagine a time when I'd want to stop working outside the home. But that time came. It's still here. I see now that my ability to work isn't limited to one season of my life. My ability to teach our children to read, however, is.

get married

APPENDIX 2

RECOMMENDED READING

de Silva, Alvaro, ed. *Brave New Family: G.K. Chesterton on Men & Women, Children, Sex, Divorce, Marriage & the Family.* San Francisco: Ignatius, 1990.

Crittenden, Danielle. *What Our Mothers Didn't Tell Us: Why Happiness Eludes the Modern Woman.* New York: Simon & Schuster, 1999.

Eggerichs, Dr. Emerson. *Love and Respect: The Love She Most Desires, The Respect He Desperately Needs.* Nashville: Integrity, 2004.

Gilder, George. *Men and Marriage.* Gretna, LA: Pelican Publishing, revised and expanded, 1986.

Kass, Amy A., and Leon R. Kass. *Wing to Wing, Oar to Oar: Readings on Courting and Marrying.* Notre Dame: Univ. Notre Dame 2000.

Maken, Debbie. *Getting Serious about Getting Married: Rethinking the Gift of Singleness.* Wheaton: Crossway, 2006.

Piper, John, and Justin Taylor, eds. *Sex and the Supremacy of Christ.* Wheaton: Crossway, 2005.

Rothman, Ellen K. *Hands and Hearts: A History of Courtship in America,* Cambridge, MA and London: Harvard Univ., reprint, 1984.

Shalit, Wendy. *A Return to Modesty: Discovering the Lost Virtue.* New York: Free Press, 1999.

Stanley, Scott M. *The Power of Commitment: A Guide to Active, Lifelong Love.* San Francisco: Jossey-Bass, 2005.

Thomas, Gary. *Sacred Marriage: What if God Designed Marriage to Make Us Holy More Than to Make Us Happy?* Grand Rapids: Zondervan, 2000.

Waite, Linda J., and Maggie Gallagher. *The Case for Marriage: Why Married People are Happier, Healthier, and Better Off Financially.* New York: Broadway Books, 2000.

Whitehead, Barbara Dafoe. *Why There Are No Good Men Left.* New York: Broadway Books, 2003.

Wilson, Douglas. *Her Hand in Marriage: Biblical Courtship in the Modern World.* Moscow, ID: Canon Press 1997.

NOTES

INTRODUCTION: THE PROFESSOR'S GRENADE

1. David Popenoe and Barbara Dafoe Whitehead, *State of Our Unions 2006: The Social Health of Marriage in America* (Piscataway: Rutgers, State Univ. New Jersey), 16.

2. Dr. Allan C. Carlson, "Marriage on Trial: Why We Must Privilege and Burden the Traditional Marriage Bond," Family Policy Lectures, Family Research Council, archived on April 18, 2006, http://www.frc.org/get.cfm?i=PL03D1.

3. Popenoe and Whitehead, *State of Our Unions*, 16.

4. Lev Grossman, "Grow Up? Not So Fast," *Time*, Sunday, January 16, 2005, http://www.time.com/time/magazine/article/0,9171,1018089,00.html.

5. Leon R. Kass, M.D., "The End of Courtship (Part 1)," September 23, 2002, http://www.aei.org/publications/filter.all,pubID.14833/pub_detail.asp.

CHAPTER 1: BELIEVE MARRIAGE IS A WORTHWHILE AND HOLY PURSUIT

1. Del Tackett, *The Truth Project* (Colorado Springs: Focus on the Family, 2006), lesson 7.

2. Charles F. Pfeiffer and Everett F. Harrison, eds., *The Wycliffe Bible Commentary* (Chicago: Moody, 1962), 5.

3. Ellen Johnson Varughese, *The Freedom to Marry: Seven Dynamic Steps to Marriage Readiness* (San Diego: Joy Press, 1992), 35.

4.   Linda J. Waite and Maggie Gallagher, *The Case for Marriage: Why Married People Are Happier, Healthier, and Better Off Financially* (New York: Broadway Books, 2000), 30.

5.   Stephen L. Nock, *Marriage in Men's Lives* (New York: Oxford, 1998), 6–7.

6.   Waite and Gallager, *The Case for Mariage*, 25.

7.   Ibid., 79.

8.   Francis de Sales, *Thy Will Be Done: Letters to Persons in the World* (Manchester, NH: Sophia Institute, 1995), 42.

9.   http://rockymtncsm.blogspot.com.

10. John MacArthur, *The MacArthur Study Bible* (Nashville: Nelson Bibles, 2006), 1706.

11. Center for Disease Control "Fertility, Contraception, and Fatherhood: Data on Men and Women from Cycle 6 (2002) of the National Survey of Family Growth, series 23, no. 26 (PHS) 2006–1978," table 22, 53, http://www.cdc.gov/nchs/data/series/sr_23/sr23_026.pdf.
     Table indicates that only 23 percent of males raised in Fundamentalist Protestant homes waited until the month of their marriage to have their first sexual intercourse—with the remaining 77 percent having sex prior to marriage.

12. MacArthur, *The MacArthur Study Bible*, 1708.

13. George Barna, *Single Focus* (Ventura: Regal Books, 2003), 89.

14. Gary Thomas, *Sacred Marriage: What if God Designed Marriage to Make Us Holy More Than to Make Us Happy?* (Grand Rapids: Zondervan, 2000).

15. David Popenoe and Barbara Dafoe Whitehead, "Life Without Children," *State of Our Unions 2006: The Social Health of Marriage in America* (Piscataway, NJ: Rutgers, The State University of New Jersey), 14.

CHAPTER 2: RESTORE BIBLICAL HONOR AND DESIRE

1. Chip Heath and Dan Heath, *Made to Stick* (New York: Random House, 2007), 98.

2. *Address to Convocation by Mother Teresa of Calcutta.* http://www.ualberta.ca/ALUMNI/history/speeches/82autteresa.htm.

3. David Popenoe and Barbara Dafoe Whitehead, 26. Norval Glenn, "With This Ring . . . A National Survey on Marriage in America," National Fatherhood Initiative, 2005, 34.

4. John MacArthur, *The MacArthur Study Bible* (Nashville: Nelson Bibles, 2006), 1806.

5. C. S. Lewis, *The Weight of Glory* (New York: Macmillan, 1980), 3–4.

6. Ibid., 4.

CHAPTER 3: MEN AREN'T JERKS, THEY'RE FALLEN (LIKE YOU)

1. Amy A. Kass and Leon R. Kass, *Wing to Wing, Oar to Oar: Readings on Courting and Marrying* (Notre Dame: Univ. Notre Dame, 2000), 2.

2. Ibid., 2.

3. Linda J. Waite and Maggie Gallagher, *The Case for Marriage: Why Married People Are Happier, Healthier, and Better Off Financially* (New York: Broadway Books, 2000), 34.

4. Ibid., 183.

5. Ibid., 176.

6. http://www.jenabbas.com/book/.

7. While "82 percent of female high school seniors and 70 percent of male say marriage is extremely important; only 64 percent of female respondents and 57 percent of male think they'll stay married." David Popenoe and Barbara Dafoe Whitehead, *State of Our Unions 2006: The Social Health of Marriage in America* (Piscataway, NJ: Rutgers, State Univ. New Jersey), figures 14 and 15, 26.

8. Del Tackett, *The Truth Project* (Colorado Springs: Focus on the Family, 2006), overview.

9. Francis A. Schaeffer, *The Great Evangelical Disaster*, (Westchester, IL: 1984, Crossway, 137).

10. Norval Glenn, "With This Ring . . . A National Survey on Marriage in America," National Fatherhood Initiative, 2005, 34.

CHAPTER 4: GOD'S STILL IN THE BUSINESS OF MAKING GOOD MATCHES

1. Barbara Mouser, *Prayer Challenge 2007*, (Waxahachie: International Council for Gender Studies, 2007).

2. http://www.christianchallenge.org/departingupc/DU013.html.

3. Barbara Dafoe Whitehead, *Why There Are No Good Men Left: The Romantic Plight of the New Single Woman* (New York: Broadway Books, 2003), 23.

4. Barbara Mouser, *Five Aspects of Woman* (Waxahachie: International Council for Gender Studies, 2002), 24.

5. Gene Edward Veith Jr., *God at Work: Your Christian Vocation in All of Life* (Wheaton: Crossway, 2002), 13–14. Used by permission of Crossway Books, a publishing ministry of Good News Publishers, Wheaton, Ill., 60187, www.crossway.org.

CHAPTER 5: YOU NEED A NETWORK

1. David Popenoe and Barbara Dafoe Whitehead, "Why Men Won't Commit," *The State of Our Unions* (Piscataway, NJ: Rutgers, The State University of New Jersey, 2002), 12–13.

2. Sharon Jayson, "Most Americans have had premarital sex, study finds," *USA Today*, 12/19/2006.

3. Miriam Grossman, *Unprotected*. "Forty years ago we had two sexually transmitted infections to worry about—now we have twenty-five." (Sentinel, the Penguin Group, New York, 2006).

4. David Wilkerson, "It's Reaping Time in America," 2000, http://www.worldchallenge.org/pulpit_series/archive/ps88_1219.html.

5. Leon R. Kass, M.D., "The End of Courtship (Part 1)," September 23, 2002, http://www.aei.org/publications/filter.all,pubID.14833/pub_detail.asp.

6. David Popenoe and Barbara Dafoe Whitehead, "Ten Important Research Findings on Marriage and Choosing a Marriage Partner," November 2004, 1, http://marriage.rutgers.edu/Publications/pubtenthingsyoungadults.htm.

7. Bobb Biehl, *Mentoring: How to Find a Mentor and How to Become One* (Lake Mary, FL: Aylen, 2005), 111–112.

8. George Barna, *Single Focus* (Ventura: Regal, 2003), 89.

CHAPTER 6: WAKING A GREAT SLEEPER

1. http://www.barna.org/FlexPage.aspx?Page=BarnaUpdate&BarnaUpdateID=47.

2. http://www.infoplease.com/ipa/A0193922.html.

3. Data from Census Bureau's 2004 American Community Survey reported that there were 29,561,000 never-married men and 23,655,000 never-married women in the United States, http://www.census.gov/acs/www/. http://factfinder.census.gov/servlet/DatasetMainPageServlet?_program=ACS&_lang=en&_ts=143547961449.

4. These are among several other cities that scored high in a recent Census Bureau report on the ratio of unmarried men 15 to 44 years per 100 unmarried women 15 to 44 years, http://factfinder.census.gov/servlet/GCTTable?_bm=y&geo_id=&parsed=true&-ds_name=ACS_2005_EST_G00_&_lang=en&format=US-35&-t_name=ACS_2005_EST_G00_GCT1203_US35&-CONTEXT=gct.

5. Lee Rainie and Mary Madden, "Not Looking for Love: Romance in America," Pew Internet and American Life Project (February 13, 2006), http://pewresearch.org/pubs/1/not-looking-for-love.

6. Center for Disease Control, "Fertility, Contraception, and Fatherhood: Data on Men and Women from Cycle 6 (2002) of the National Survey of Family Growth," series 23, no. 26 (PHS) 2006–1978. Tables 37–38, pp. 68–69, http://www.cdc.gov/nchs/data/series/sr_23/sr23_026.pdf.

What follows is a comparison of the percentage of men and women 15–44 years of age who either agree or strongly agree with the statement, "It is better to get married than to go through life being single," according to selected characteristics.

Total males—65.8%
Total females—50.6%

Fundamentalist Protestant males—68%
Fundamentalist Protestant females—59.3%

Males to whom religion is very important—73.6%
Females to whom religion is very important—57%

Males to whom religion is not very important—56.9%
Females to whom religion is not very important—38.7%

Notice that the percentage of men to whom religion is not very important comes in just 0.1% behind females who say religion is very important in their agreement on getting married vs. going through life single.

7. http://www.boundless.org/2005/articles/a0001409.cfm.
8. http://www.boundless.org/2005/articles/a0001306.cfm.

CHAPTER 7: PULLING A RUTH

1. Debbie Maken, *Getting Serious about Getting Married: Rethinking the Gift of Singleness* (Wheaton: Crossway, 2006), 160.

CHAPTER 8: LIVING LIKE YOU'RE PLANNING TO MARRY

1. "In a survey . . . by the National Association of Home Builders, builders and architects predicted that more than 60 percent of custom houses would have dual master bedrooms by 2015," Tracie Rozhon, "To Have, Hold, and Cherish, Until Bedtime," *New York Times*, March 11, 2007.

2. Between student loan debt and consumer debt, new graduates enter the job market with an average credit load of $23,000: $19,200 in student loan debt and $3,000 in unpaid credit card balances. From Kelli B. Grant, "Get a Handle on School Debt," *Wall Street Journal Online*, June 3, 2007; and John E. Waites, "Bankruptcy Court Working to Prevent Credit Mistakes," *The Post and Courier*, June 6, 2007, http://www.charleston.net/news/2007/jun/06/bankruptcy_

court_working_prevent_credit_mistakes/.
According to the Public Interest Research Group's Higher Education Project, 39 percent of new graduates with loans carry an "unmanageable debt," defined as requiring payments of 8 percent or more of the borrower's monthly income", http://www.ncpa.org/iss/soc/2003/pd010903e.html.

3. http://www.ncpa.org/iss/soc/2003/pd010903e.html. Source: Allan Carlson, "The Anti-Dowry: A Complaint about Our Student Loan System," *Weekly Standard*, December 16, 2002.

4. "[Couples who] marry later in life . . . may have more adjusting to do when it comes to merging partners' finances. Prior to marriage at an older age, individuals are accustomed to making money decisions without having to consider another person." From a survey of 21,501 married couples from all fifty states. "National Survey of Marital Strengths," PREPARE-ENRICH, 1999, 11, http://www.prepare-enrich.com/files/Article_Info/national_survey.pdf.

5. Jay Teachman, "Premarital Sex, Premarital Cohabitation, and the Risk of Subsequent Marital Dissolution among Women," *Journal of Marriage and the Family*, 65 (2003), 444–455, http://www.ncfr.org/pdf/press_releases/PRESS%20RELEAS2.pdf.
This study did imply that women who cohabit or have sex only with their future husbands incur no discernible increased risk of divorce. The problem, however, is that you can't know until you marry him if the guy you're sleeping with will become your husband. And divorce isn't the only negative consequence to consider.

6. http://www.boundless.org/1999/features/a0000028.html.

7. Wendy Shalit, *A Return to Modesty* (New York: Free Press, 1999), 212.

8. Dr. James Dobson, *Romantic Love: How to Be Head Over Heels and Still Land on Your Feet* (Ventura: Regal, 2004), 39–40.

9. Danielle Crittenden, *What Our Mothers Didn't Tell Us: Why Happiness Eludes the Modern Woman* (New York: Simon & Schuster, 1999), 65–66.

10. www.boundless.org/2005/articles/a0001541.cfm.

11. Barry Schwartz, *The Paradox of Choice: Why More Is Less* (New York: Ecco, 2004), 38–39.

12. Barbara Dafoe Whitehead, *Why There Are No Good Men Left: The Romantic Plight of the New Single Woman* (New York: Broadway Books, 2003), 64–65, 76.

13. David Popenoe and Barbara Dafoe Whitehead, "Who Wants to Marry a Soul Mate?: New Survey Findings on Young Adults' Attitudes about Love and Marriage," *The State of Our Unions* (2001), 14, http://marriage.rutgers.edu/Publications/SOOU/TEXTSOOU2001.htm.

14. Ibid., 13–14.

15. Polly Shulman, "Great Expectations," *Psychology Today*, March 2004, http://psychologytoday.com/articles/pto-20040301-000002.html.

16. Ibid., 6.

17. Crittenden, *What Our Mothers Didn't Tell Us*, 64.

18. C. S. Lewis, *The Four Loves* (San Diego: Harcourt Brace Jovanovich, 1960), 169.

19. Alex Kendrick, *Facing the Giants*, (Sony Pictures, 2007).

CHAPTER 9: PRAY BOLDLY

1. John MacArthur, *The MacArthur Study Bible* (Nashville: Nelson Bibles, 2006), 1519.

2. Walter Wangerin Jr., *Little Lamb, Who Made Thee?* (New York: HarperPaperbacks, 1993), 65–66.

3. http://www.boundless.org/departments/theophilus/a0000978.html.

APPENDIX: COMMONLY ASKED QUESTIONS

1. "Women now make up 56 percent of the college population—and that number continues to rise. Within ten years, three million more women than men could be attending college" http://www.pbs.org/newshour/extra/features/july-dec02/college.html.

2. I'm thankful to Douglas Wilson's book *Her Hand in Marriage* for helping me understand this aspect of biblical submission.

andice Watters was experiencing the relationship frustration so common among Christian women until she was hit with the "get married" message while in graduate school. It changed her perspective and her approach, and led to a much-desired change in her marital status. Whether in countless e-mails from *Boundless* (*boundless.org*) readers, audience surveys, sociological research, or popular relationship books, over the past ten years, she has seen the widespread need for and validation of this message.

Candice earned her M.A. in public policy from Regent University where she met and married Steve Watters. After graduating, they moved to Colorado to work with Focus on the Family. In 1998, they founded *Boundless.org*, a Webzine for singles in college and beyond. Candice served as its editor for four years. Now she writes regularly for the site about courtship and dating, getting married, and figuring out where kids fit into it all. Additionally, she answers questions from readers in "Boundless Answers: Women," a biweekly advice column. Steve is the director of young adults ministries for Focus on the Family. The Watters have three children.

To join the Women Praying Boldly community or to e-mail the author with questions or comments, or speaking requests, please visit the *Get Married* website at www.helpgetmarried.com.

For the woman who hasn't had any dating opportunities come her way, for the woman who has just hit another relational dead-end, and for the woman who is watching the relationship she's in get bogged down …

There's still hope

If you're ready to live like you're planning to marry, visit www.helpgetmarried.com.

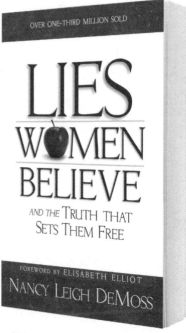

OVER ONE-THIRD MILLION SOLD

LIES WOMEN BELIEVE

AND THE TRUTH THAT SETS THEM FREE

FOREWORD BY ELISABETH ELLIOT

NANCY LEIGH DEMOSS

ISBN-13: 978-0-8024-7296-0

Bestselling author of *Lies Women Believe*

NANCY LEIGH DEMOSS

Delete

CHOOSING

Forgiveness

Your Journey to Freedom

FOREWORD BY DAVID JEREMIAH

ISBN-13: 978-0-8024-3251-3
Paperback Available April 2008
ISBN-13: 978-0-8024-3253-7

We are like Eve. We have all experienced defeats and failures, trouble and turmoil. And we ache to do things over, to have lives of harmony and peace. Nancy Leigh DeMoss exposes those areas of deception most commonly believed by Christian women. She sheds light on how we can be delivered from bondage and set free to walk in God's grace, forgiveness, and abundant life. The book offers the most effective weapon to counter and overcome Satan's deceptions –God's truth.

God forgiving as we do? That's a scary thought. Leading author and radio host Nancy Leigh DeMoss explains how forgiving like God is a choice that frees us from the burdens of bitterness, anger, and isolation. Women and men struggling with long-held hurts will be helped and healed by Nancy's wisdom and God's truth.

by Nancy Leigh DeMoss
Find it now at your favorite local or online bookstore.

www.MoodyPublishers.com

and the
Bride Wore
White

Seven Secrets to Sexual Purity

DANNAH GRESH

ISBN-13: 978-0-8024-8342-3

Dannah Gresh's *And the Bride Wore White* exposes our culture's lies about sex, and prepares young women for the world's pressures. This special addition includes dozens of stories/personal testimonies of hurt and healing ... first time salvations ... confessions to parents that lead to accountability ... and lots of wedding proposals, of course.

Training materials available for the bestselling *And the Bride Wore White* by Dannah Gresh. Perfect for individual and small group study. In a warm, revealing style, Dannah shows her own story of joy and heartache. Included are interviews and insights from well known writers, speakers, and musicians.

by Dannah Gresh
Find it now at your favorite local or online bookstore.

www.MoodyPublishers.com